THE MAGIC OF LOVE

Our gratitude is extended to Elsie Armor
for her permission to reprint this book.

Other books by the author:

Ernest Holmes, the Man

Change Your Thinking, Change Your Life
(co-authored with Ernest Holmes)

The Magic Of Love

Including Practical Meditations
for Using Its Healing Power

Reginald C. Armor

ISBN: 0-917849-14-0
Library of Congress Catalog Card Number: 67-14304

Printed in the United States of America

Science of Mind Communications
3251 West Sixth Street
Los Angeles, California 90020

To my wife Elsie for her loving understanding
through these many years,

To my lifelong friend the late Ernest Holmes
for his inspiration and guidance,

To my many students and associates for their
stimulating interest and inspiration,

This book is lovingly dedicated.

"The greatest happiness of life is the conviction that we are loved, loved for ourselves, or rather, loved in spite of ourselves."

— VICTOR HUGO

Contents

Introduction: Let's Get Acquainted

Who am I? What am I? Why do I act as I do? What is my purpose in life, and where am I going?

No, this is not a quiz contest, but unquestionably these are some of the most important questions that are uppermost in everyone's mind. We have sought answers, some of which have been satisfactory while others have not. As thinking beings, we have the ability to choose, and it is our nature constantly to seek the *reasons*, *whys*, and *wherefores* of *existence*. To lose an inquisitive interest in ourselves, others, and life itself, is to begin to hibernate or vegetate. This is contrary to the nature of humankind; for we are not plants, neither are we animals of the type that periodically lose contact with life through long hibernation. For us to lose interest in life simply means, literally, to *cease to live*.

As intelligent beings, we are aware that it would be impossible for us to know all the answers to everything. Should this be possible, an impasse would be reached that would be just as boring as it would be if we stopped asking questions. No more fields to conquer. No more horizons to be scanned. Nothing to look forward to in anticipation. With this state of mind and affairs, one would actually be "bored to death." It seems as though Truth is always a two-edged sword, a paradox, with the searcher always riding on the "horns of dilemma"; on the one hand, an inner urge or drive to know more and more — and on the other hand, the logical assumption that we shall never know it all. Psychologically, this situation provides the basis for a good old-fashioned inferiority complex or a whopping big case of frustration, either of which can be damaging to one's ego and to one's happy expression of life.

In this connection, I am reminded of an incident that happened during counseling. We had been talking of our need to ever expand our understanding and find answers to questions that constantly come up and at the same time realize that we will never know all the answers. Suddenly the one to whom I was talking looked squarely at me and said, "Gee, Doc, that seems pretty futile—like walking on a treadmill, never getting anywhere. We sure have our work cut out for us. It's quite a job—living, thinking, and trying to figure things out. Seems to me it would be a lot simpler and easier if we were cats and dogs. Then we would not have to think, because it would all be done for us and instinct would take the place of thinking."

Well, we had a good laugh about it and seriously decided that in spite of everything we would still rather be human beings, for who in their right mind would want to lead a dog's life? Besides, we don't have much to do about the matter. Some Power, in Its wisdom, created the dog to lead his life and us to lead *ours*, so we decided what was done was done, and we would just have to go on from there. All of which seems to be a good philosophic approach to the subject.

Our need to know the answers to questions prompted by our inner urge to learn more about ourselves, life, and where we fit into the overall scheme of things and where we go from here must be satisfied in some manner. This seems to be self-evident. It also is just as self-evident that we will never know all the answers, for to do so would mean that we had encompassed Infinity. This of itself would be impossible, for if the Infinite could be encompassed or completely understood, it would mean a completed Infinite, which is a contradiction of terms.

Well, here we are again where we started, faced with an inner urge (over which we seem to have little if any control) for answers to basic questions and needs dealing with our existence. Let us approach the subject simply and right where we live. Let us not add to our frustration by too much abstract thought and get a headache by feeling guilty because we apparently cannot know the unknowable.

Obviously, if we cannot know all the answers, we must know enough of them to satisfy us at any given time. If this can be done, we have left room for growth and forward-looking enthusiasm, provided we are really satisfied with this position. But as someone has aptly said, "Thereby hangs a tale." It is not easy to admit to ourselves or say to another, on being asked for information, "I really don't know," and be completely free from a feeling of guilt. Usually one's ego or at least that part of it which may be inflated, gets in the way. We may misinterpret the urge to grow in understanding and feel frustrated and guilty if we don't know it all.

We shall have arrived at a certain state of maturity if, on being asked something—the answer to which we do not know—we can with no inner feeling of guilt say, "Really, I don't know."

Maybe we will have to work with ourselves on this problem, because it is so essential if we are to be good to ourselves and realize the "approval of self" so necessary to a happy life. Maybe a solution could be found in the story of the little boy who said to his playmate, "Me and my brother Tom, we know everything." Whereupon one of his pals responded, "I don't believe it."

"It's true," said the little boy, "just try me out."

"O.K.," said his pal, "if you're so smart, tell me this—why is it that a black hen with a red comb can lay a brown egg with a yellow yolk?"

After scratching his head for some time, the little boy, quite unembarrassed, said, "Golly, that must be one of the things my brother Tom knows."

This little boy really believed what he said. He had faith in his brother's knowledge and was not in the least embarrassed by his answer. Nothing could convince him that he had not stated the case correctly. No frustration or self-condemnation here. His mind was left free and open to move on to the next idea, and in the mind of a little child there are many fields to conquer and wonders to explore. It is true that because of his limited experience he did not realize that his logic was not quite correct. He had not yet accepted the all too prevalent attitude that there were many things he could not do, so why make the effort, why try? Experience had not yet dampened his faith in life and enthusiasm for living.

Does this faith and enthusiasm have to be shattered by the growing-up process? If experience invites wisdom and wisdom invites mature ideas and new experiences, why should we not be able to carry over into adult life the basic ideas that are so helpful in the little child?

It is true that someday our little boy will know that his brother is not all-wise, but wisdom will tell him that the necessary answers to questions are available when they are really needed. It may be that his faith will be transferred to some other individual or group of individuals, only to be transferred to others, as his mature thinking leads him to realize that those persons whom he has placed on a pedestal have "feet of clay."

The important thing is that the faith and enthusiasm about life shall be kept intact. If this is diminished, something within the self begins to close in upon us. We become frustrated and begin to lose, in some measure, our zest for living. We have been told that "...except ye become as little children, ye shall not enter into the kingdom of heaven." (Matt. 18:3) How true this is. We need the spontaneity, joyousness, exuberance, vitality, and wonder of the little child to fully enjoy life and really live. And yet we know that the child must grow up and realize that perhaps his unthinking logic has contained flaws. No doubt this is what prompted the Wise One to say also, "...Except a man be born again, he cannot see the kingdom of God." (John 3:3) Again, we have the paradox of Truth. But while truth often seems to be a two-edged sword, logic based on mature wisdom tells us that basic truth could never be founded on duality. Could black be white? Water be dry? Or hatred be love? Yet how often our relative thinking based on snap judgment would lead us to suppose that such might be the case.

It is true that the child in us must be born again into a seeming new world of mature thinking and experience, and a part of this growing-up process is to carry over into any new experience the faith, trust, and enthusiasm of living. Wisdom seems to be a necessary connecting link on the road to maturity. Wisdom goes beyond apparent facts and penetrates the reason for facts. Wisdom pierces the unseen world of causes and reveals a whole new world of possibility and adventure. Wisdom gets us out of the limiting ruts of yesterday's thinking and reveals new fields to conquer. Wisdom can sustain the enthusiasm and faith of the little boy whose feeling of faith has not yet been shaken by doubt as he moves into mature experiences.

So the inner urge to find answers and move forward persists in the mind of each of us, no matter what our chronological age may be. Satisfying answers must be forthcoming if we are to receive the maximum of joy of living at all times. This desire for joy and satisfaction in living is not a selfish one, or it would not have been born with us and be so persistent in the hearts of all humankind. If we are honest with ourselves, we will admit this to be true, and if we are good to ourselves we will seek with all that we are to do something about it.

It is the purpose of this book to reveal some of the ways that will make this journey of mature self-discovery practical and fruitful. This discovery must be made by the self. But this does not mean by the individualized self alone. Remember the little boy's brother. In his childlike approach to his problem, the little boy's answer, "That must be one of the things my brother knows," was his solution to the problem. No doubt his statement was prompted by an instinctive realization that "no man lives unto himself alone."

The ideas expressed here are not new. Perhaps it could be said that they are individual applications of ideas as old as time itself. That they have proved helpful in the lives of so many in eliminating the pitfalls of immature thinking and thus lessened the chances of unhappy experiences, gives them vital meaning. These ideas, helpful in easing the frustrations of living, are based on my own experience and also the experiences of the many hundreds of persons I have talked to and worked with over a period of many years.

There is no royal road to freedom. All roads based on wisdom and determination, however, will lead one in the right direction. All the answers are not in this book, but enough of them are here to stimulate one's mind in such a way that he or she may more freely advance on the pathway of self-discovery in response to the inner urge within every person. We have tried to approach the subject from a broad-gauged point of view, one that embodies ideas with which each shall in a large measure be in agreement. The findings of psychology, philosophy, science, and religion are emphasized, for are these not outstanding guideposts along the pathway of life? Religion plays an important role in the life of humankind. We are not speaking of any particular creed or dogma but of the general idea involved in a religious approach to life. All religions are basically good in that they seek to acquaint humankind with its innate nature and seek to supply some of the answers to the hows and whys of life and living. The same thing may be said about the sciences and philosophies. While this is true, the warmth of human kindness and understanding also needs to be added in these approaches to Truth. Wherever we find true wisdom in any of these methods of searching for a mature appraisal of life, to that degree will we find warmth of inner agreement with it. It is our thesis that wisdom is true understanding and true understanding is the principal attribute of love. Love is the seeming miracle that makes life meaningful. It is the power that, if accepted and practiced, smooths the way for each step on our road to maturity.

Understanding love will transform the faith of the little child in his brother or sister and expand it to include a faith in life and a Power and Presence in and through life that really does know all the answers. True wisdom, expressed as understanding love, will, as little children grow in experience, lead them to realize that all people are our brothers and sisters. But wisdom will not be content to let them stop there but will lead them to know that because this is so there is a common source from which all spring. That each exists because of a Power greater than they are and each is one with this Power is the ultimate of faith based on understanding love. This should be the basis for any inquiry into Truth, be it science, philosophy, or religion. But this alone is not enough. Each of us must make the Truth our own. We must feel the power of faith. We must use it. We must accept that which seems reasonable to us and begin to make such wisdom effective in our lives. As we let understanding love guide us, the so-called miracle of love to accomplish for us and through us becomes apparent. As you read the printed pages of this book, "make it a thing of joy." Be as relaxed and free from tension or strain as possible. Do not be frustrated by feeling you have to know all the answers. No one ever does. No one ever will. It may be that you will want to read the summations at the end of each chapter first. It may be that you will find it helpful to skip to the specific ideas embodied in the meditations in Part II. It may be that you will want to begin at the beginning and read straight through to the end of the book. Follow your inner urge as you pick up this book. The way you decide will be the best for you. The important thing is to read with an open mind. Feel that through your efforts something good is going to happen to you.

The power for good is never in the word, whether spoken or

printed. These are but symbols seeking to express thoughts, ideas, and feelings. They are necessary symbols, however, in our day-to-day communications with life. Your own personal reaction to an inner feeling about the word is what counts. The value of communication is that it stimulates our own minds and thought processes to expand our own awareness. This is how we grow. Each advance in wisdom enables us to achieve a greater feeling of dominion over our own thoughts and experiences of living. There may be ideas in this book with which you may not wholeheartedly agree. There, no doubt, will be many that will meet with your complete approval. Some of the ideas you may wish to lay aside for the moment, to take up at a later time. This is what we mean by reading with an open mind.

Read on, and may you be blessed in your adventure. It is my fervent hope that you will find many ideas that will be the means of opening new vistas of thought and feeling that will lead to an ever-increasing joy, assurance, and enthusiasm in your life.

—R.C.A.

Part One

1　The Magic Of Love

"Love is always in the mood of believing in miracles."

–J.C. Powys

Have you ever been in love?

"Yes," you may say, "but isn't that a foolish question, for is it not true that everyone experiences love in some degree in his or her life?" However, if your experience with love has been largely on the emotional level, you may say, "Sure, I have been in love many times, and I have fallen out of love just as many times." You may even feel it is something over which you, with your intellect, have little control.

It may come as quite a surprise and somewhat of a shock to realize that in spite of appearances, there is an underlying basic law of balance and harmony governing all of life's activities. Could we not say that by its very nature, we may call this the Law of Love? If this is so, if one could more completely understand this basic law, its nature, and how it functions, one could through conscious cooperation with it, receive more of its wonderful benefits. Who is there who does not deeply desire more love to come into their life?

A Wise One has said, "All is Love, yet all is Law." It has also been said that the Law of the Lord is perfect. Observing the activities of life or nature, we witness a balanced and harmonious action constantly taking place throughout the universe. We also observe in the so-called material world as the scientists turn their attention inward to the atomic structure, a purposiveness and balanced law and order at work.

As we think of the term *love*, we think of harmony, beauty, and balance. As we see harmony, beauty and balance as the governing factors of God's Universe, as we become aware of the wisdom and careful provision for the sustaining of each creation, as we think of the wonderful creative and recreative power within the human body, who can say that the basic Law of the Lord is not perfect?

From a lack of understanding of this basic law of harmony and beauty that underlies all of life and its activities, arises the possibility of the problems of life—its fears, frustrations, and unlovely experiences.

It is widely believed and accepted that love is a synonym for God. If God is love, the more one can understand the nature of love and put that understanding into practice, the more God-like will be one's experience. Do we believe God is love? If we do, more love will be ours as we contemplate the verities of God. But how are we to do this? It will help if we think in terms of a law of love that, when understood, can increasingly be used for our benefit.

In consciously using the law of love to experience an increased good, it is important to keep our thinking clear as well as affirmative. For instance, as we observe poverty, sickness, inharmony, confusion, loneliness, and those things that make life at times anything but lovely, we may be tempted to say there must be a basic law of inharmony as well as harmony. But this, logically, could not be. Two laws in action opposed to each other would cancel each other out. There must be, and is, a more logical explanation for the apparent "pairs of opposites" of experience.

In dealing with any natural law, the more we understand and, through cooperation with its nature, use it, the greater good we derive from that law. This is true of the law of love.

As we consider love to be a basic law of life and the Universe, and as we come to understand and cooperate with it according to its nature, we become more and more the recipients of the greater good that has been lovingly provided by an Infinite Wisdom that we call God. Through the understanding eyes of love, inharmony is seen to be but a lack of harmony, and hatred, envy and jealousy are only evidences of a lack of love. These are not the offspring of unhealthy negative laws but rather results of a misuse, an unwise use, or no use at all of the basic law of love. Truly, love is a synonym for God, and the Law of the Lord is perfect. "Hell is created but for the lack of an understanding of Heaven."

One of the principal attitudes of mind that keeps us from expressing more love in our life is fear. Fear, also, is not a power of and by itself but rather an absence of faith or understanding. We learn to conquer our fears through a greater understanding of that which we fear. A wise or cautious approach to fear will remove its sting. Understanding is a synonym for love. The more we seek to understand ourself, the less we will fear our motives and certain less desirable things that we felt to be true about ourself. Self-understanding supplies the tools of self-dominion when applied in a determined manner. Self-appreciation logically follows self-dominion. Fear of self, so common to most of us at times, cannot exist in this atmosphere. Also, the more we understand others' motives, frailties, weaknesses, the less fear we have of people. Consequently, the less fear we have for life. "Thou shalt love thy neighbor as thyself." (Matt. 22:39) Love moves in as fear disappears, because it was there all the time—just covered up. Permitting understanding or love to move into our thinking about people and life opens the way for the basic law of love to dominate our thoughts and actions. As we come to understand God as the loving Presence, the creating and sustaining Power of the Universe, we can in no-wise fear God. Through this understanding, we learn to trust and to love God. Surely the warmth and glow of love dominates our thinking as we understand ourselves to a greater degree. In this understanding, we recognize that as individuals we have the power of choice, and as a result of our choices, things happen to us, both in our minds and in our external affairs. As we think of the less desirable things we have permitted to happen in the past, we fear them less and less as we realize that we have merely chosen unwisely. Now we can choose more wisely. Likewise in our associations with others, as we come to understand ourselves and mentally place ourselves in the position of another, we understand more clearly their motive. In this way, the power of understanding love becomes a factor in our relationship with people. We may not like everything another does but neither do we have to hate or fear them. We may even learn to love the real person beneath the exterior in which they have encased themself.

Recognizing that love is governed by law, we have the tools at hand whereby we may change a seeming lack of love in any department of our life. We can limit our use of the law of electricity through an ignorant or noncooperative attitude toward electricity. This is true in connection with our use of any natural law. It is definitely true of our use of the law of love. Many of the attitudes of mind that keep the law of love from moving in and through our life more completely are envy, jealousy, fear, misunderstanding and confusion of mind. These are mental attitudes that we may continue to accept or that we may change at any time by choosing to cooperate more fully with the law of love.

If we are to remove fear, envy, jealousy and those things that frustrate and keep us from expressing joy and enthusiasm for living, we must free our minds of these negative ideas. We do this by a definite, persistent and systematic focusing of our attention on those things that we would call lovely. The place to begin is within the self, in our thinking. The time to begin is *right now*.

We have been admonished to love our neighbor *as* ourselves. This implies that we must first love ourselves. This is not an egotistical attitude of mind, because as "sons of the Most High," in spite of any evidence to the contrary, we can love the true God-self that is our Real self. To the degree that we love our God-self, to that degree can we love the God-self in every person we contact. Through the eyes of understanding love we see ourselves in a new light, freed from self-condemnation, forgiving ourselves for past and less wise choices and giving our attention to those things that are of value and that are true. We can always find something about ourselves to love and praise if we look earnestly and diligently. Likewise, a friendly and warm atmosphere in our daily contact with others is felt as we realize that we can love the real God-intended person in each, even though we do not like everything he or she may do or say. We see each as a Divine being, endowed with freedom of choice.

Everyone is experiencing according to their choices, even as you and I. As we understand this, we respect the Divine origin of all persons and love them even though they, at times, make unwise decisions, even as you and I. As we persistently seek to sense the presence of love, expressing in and through all nature and in and through us each individually, our awareness of love ceases to be an intellectual concept only and becomes an emotional acceptance as well. Our mental attitudes begin to change. Less desirable thought patterns dissolve. As we love our neighbors as ourselves, unconscious affirmative communication is established that permits us to give and receive in a richer measure that great good within each of us awaiting our recognition so that it may pour itself generously into our experience. Thinking of the warmth and glow of understanding love as the law of love in action, we can feel secure in the knowledge that love will respond to us according to our use of and cooperation with it. Such is the *magic of love*.

As we think lovely, constructive, and harmonious thoughts and as we give our attention to the enthusiasm, the warmth of life going out from us and coming back to us as experience, there comes to us a sense of the rightness of things and an inner security. We feel more at home in this life in which we live and more kind and warm toward those whom we meet. We begin to think of ourselves as not separated from life and living. We accept our good, our joy, not in terms of something we must selfishly hang on to but as something to be shared with others. Truly, the "Law of the Lord is perfect," God-given perfection. But to be satisfying, this must all be shared with others if we are to be vital, effectual, and happy.

Watch the magic of the law of love respond—a smile returned, kind and thoughtful actions toward others coming back to you. Inwardly thrill as warmth of feeling and understanding of others returns to you as helpfulness and thoughtfulness from all sources.

Yes, there is a magic of love, the magic of the fulfilling of the law of life by which we were created and under which we live.

Do we believe it will work for us? The only way we will know is to try it. Let's begin today, *right now*, to find out for ourselves that "Love is the fulfilling of the Law."

TO SUM IT UP

All of us experience love in our life.

There is a basic law of love, just as there is a basic law of mathematics, music, chemistry, physics, etc.

The attributes of the law of love are harmony, balance, beauty, integrity, and wisdom.

Hatred, jealousy, malice, fear, frustration are mental attitudes that hinder, limit, and tend to freeze out the action of the law of love.

The law of love, as with every other law of life, responds as we use it according to its nature.

Thoughts of harmony, beauty, courage, and oneness with life neutralize the less desirable, hurtful attitudes of mind and open the way for the law of love to respond to us.

Love is a synonym for God. Good is a synonym for God.

As we use the law of love and contemplate the meaning of good, we come to understand more fully the Nature of God. This understanding permits the *Magic of Love* to go to work in every department of our living.

2 How Did I Get This Way?

*"To love is to believe, to hope, to know;
'Tis an essay, a taste of heaven below."*
—Edmond Waller

"How did I get this way?" Sound familiar? All of us, when things are not going as smoothly as they might, have asked, "Why this, or why that? How in the world did I ever get myself into this predicament? Why is it that I never seem to have quite enough money or quite enough love or friendship in my experience?" Do these questions sound familiar? If we are experiencing happy conditions and events, it is safe to say we have no pressing problem. If unhappiness, uncertainty or doubt rules our minds, however, or we feel the need for tremendous improvement in our affairs, we do have a problem, and that is to know what to do to bring about a change in our experience. Often the first step that we must take to bring this about is to acknowledge that we, in a way, have been responsible for anything that has ever happened to us. We should quickly add that much of our distress or undesirable experiences of the past or at the present time in our life have not been *consciously willed* or accepted on our part. We have, to a great extent, allowed ourselves to be victims of environment and circumstance. Often we have unwittingly let undesirable opinions of others affect us. However, the fact remains that we are the ones who are experiencing, and are the ones who must take the first step that will eliminate whatever the undesirable experience is.

An understanding that there is a law of love acting in, through, and sustaining all life, will help us greatly in taking that first step and support us in all succeeding steps. Logically, it is very easy to accept this, because we realize that if for one moment anything but law and order existed on a universal scale, we would have a tremendously confused and upset Universe, which of course would not be thinkable. Moreover, the findings of the science of astronomy and mathematics tend to prove beyond a question of doubt that there is an intelligent law and order at work through all the Universe.

If we believe that all life is governed intelligently by law and order, then we are certainly believing that nothing happens by chance. This truth will rule out any belief in fatalism. We cannot say that our undesirable experience is the result of some unstable law or is the work of some capricious power or force over which we have no control. It is very easy for us to demonstrate that "it is done unto us" according to our belief. Another way of stating it would be: There is a Law of Cause and Effect operating intelligently in all phases of life and therefore operating through each of us. This implies that for every objective experience or effect, there is an inward cause from which the objective expression springs. This Law of Cause and Effect may also be called the law of attraction as it expresses in our experience. For example, if our mind is in a happy state, we will have a tendency to see and view happiness wherever we look. We seem to attract to us happy people and happy situations. On the other hand, if our mind is gloomy, if we are upset or confused by some happening of the day, or if we are inwardly anxious, we find that our every endeavor to do things will be upset in a like manner. We can be under pressure and in a hurry to dress ourselves in the morning and find that our "fingers are all thumbs." Or, late for an evening appointment, we can be in such a hurry to get our dishes done that we become so upset through the strenuous effort and confusion that surrounds such effort that several dishes are broken. These are but simple examples of objective expression in a person's life that would result from an inner state of mind. Our inner state of mind is our inner state of awareness.

In implying that we are responsible for our experiences in life through an inner awareness, we are not saying that we would not be influenced by that which goes on around us. Each of us certainly is to a degree so influenced, but this also is a matter of our acceptance—largely an unconscious acceptance—that must consciously be recognized as such in order to intelligently do something about it. If we feel that someone is deliberately trying to influence us, as we become consciously aware of this, we can do something within our own thought that will render harmless such attempted influence. This is also true in cases of undesirable influences from any source. How can this be done? It is done by inducing within our minds a mental attitude that knows we cannot be influenced against our will or our good. For instance, we can walk into a room where there has been bickering and quarreling. Not realizing what is happening, we will, no doubt, feel in a bickering and quarreling mood ourselves. This is our privilege. On the other hand, we can walk into the same room realizing that we, through the Law of Cause and Effect, may neutralize the effect of any experience by changing our inward feeling about that which is happening. In this way we can maintain an attitude of poise. To the degree that the inward feeling is changed, so does the outward experience begin to change in an almost miraculous way. Such is the magic of the law of love. So it is that one person who knows that he or she need not be subject to a law of chance or to the opinions and beliefs of others or to anything but the law of love, actually can be the means of changing an unlovely atmosphere. Unconsciously, those persons who have been bickering would feel the presence of the law of love being recognized and applied in this particular situation. Try it as an interesting experiment the next time such a situation arises. Something has to give when the Law of Love (God) is realized and applied.

In using this understanding in our everyday living, we must not feel we have to change people in order to change conditions. We change our thought about people and about ourselves, but actually never change people themselves. We should never accept the responsibility that we must change people and change conditions through the use of our intellect or our *will power*. One does not forcefully change the darkness into light when one uses the law of electricity by pressing the button that lights the darkened room. If our premise regarding our conscious use of the Law of Cause and Effect is correct, objective appearances will automatically change as our inner state of awareness or reaction to such appearances is viewed through the light of understanding.

We should accept this ability to think and choose for ourselves as our God-intended birthright. In fact, when we say, "Others cannot influence against our desire," or, "We do not become submerged in the depths of despondency through objective appearances and happenings," we are simply affirming that, by the power of choice, we are creating a change in objective appearances and conditions through our reaction to that which goes on. If we claim this ability for ourselves, we must also know that it is true for every other individual, for we cannot completely accept our Divine prerogative of choice and, at the same time, believe that we can exercise that choice to control others. Therefore, our assertion of freedom in changing conditions will never become something that will be detrimental to others. This thought alone will create harmonious conditions in our associations with people, for each innately feels this Divine freedom within himself and instinctively rebels against anything which, or any person who, attempts to interfere with it. This is as it should be—as God intended it to be.

In bringing about a change of conditions through our inner awareness, again the magic law of love is brought into play. It takes time to change our awareness, but just as everything else that we accomplish in life takes thought, time, and practice, so we should be willing to have patience with ourselves. We must persist in our attempts to put the law of love into operation. The effort will be reflected in every department of our life. There must be a willingness to permit others to express their lives, as well as a willingness to be on the job, mentally speaking, so that we will not entertain thoughts of separation, of malice, or of hatred—those negative thoughts that are the seeds for unhappy experiences.

Watch the difference in our human relationships as we adopt toward others a permissive attitude of "you may" or "don't you think" rather than "you must" or "you will." This attitude is giving the other person the opportunity of expressing his or her freedom of choice and at the same time preserving our own.

It is not always easy to change habitual attitudes of mind. We will find over and over again that we will have to bring ourselves up short in our thinking and say, "Stop, look, and listen. Where is this reaction to this or that going to lead me? What objective experience is going to come out of this attitude of mind that I am entertaining?"

Realizing that we "got this way" largely through our reaction to an inner awareness to life and people, most of which has been *unconsciously* accepted, indicates something can be done about what we are, should we so desire. Consciously, persistently, and definitely we must use the same process by which "we got this way" to get us the way we want to be. An attitude of *allowing* rather than *forcing* the necessary changes in our inner awareness is important. This could be stated as a *willingness to let it be so*, rather than *willing* that it be so.

We will find that we may have to say over and over, "I am not going to allow this or that appearance, this person or that situation to continue to affect me. I am not going to feel that I have to run away from or ignore anything. I am going to increasingly recognize and use the basic Law of Life according to my highest understanding of its nature—harmony, balance, beauty and love. I am going to sense the magic of the law of love moving into my thinking and every aspect of my life in a harmonious and constructive and a happy way. I persist in my endeavor to have an inner awareness and an inner appreciation that life is good, that God is good, and that I and all other persons are one with and expressing this good life."

As we become increasingly aware of the good within ourselves and in every manifestation of life and that this good flows from the center of the Universe itself as the great law of love in action, we break down the barriers and the resistances to harmonious living. As we increasingly sense the law of love in and through all life, we realize that we do not live unto ourselves alone. As we seek to understand, we are understood. As we seek to help, we are helped. As we are generous, giving of ourselves and our good, so does our good return to us from any necessary source. Thus it is that we may witness love's magic in action—see those undesirable things and experiences in our life change. Don't argue with or about this *magic of love*. Embrace it, woo it, encourage it. The question may change from "How did I get this way?" to "What can I do to become the way I want to be?"

TO SUM IT UP

Everyone has problems.

Pressing problems demand adequate answers if we are to be happy. Facing the problem is the first step.

We are the ones who permit problems to affect us. However, our acceptance of problems, situations, unhappy experiences is largely an *unconscious* acceptance.

Recognition of our responsibility in acceptance of undesirable conditions causes us to realize that we can also be the way that will make such conditions change.

Fatalism, predestination, or the so-called law of averages or chance are ruled out as we accept the fact that we have consciously or *unconsciously* accepted the conditions we experience.

We solve our problems through an intelligent approach to the situation. An attitude of condemnation of self or others should be avoided.

Our inner feeling about a situation is the key to its continuation or its change. Does the situation have to persist? Can it be changed? What can be done about it?

The conscious practice of an inner awareness of love permits the *magic of love* to produce new ideas (acceptances) that will nullify the effect of those ideas (acceptances) that have produced unhappy situations and problems.

"How we got this way" is largely our own doing. What we do about the way we are—if we don't like it—is up to us.

The law of love will respond affirmatively, as does every other law of nature.

3 Our Divine Partnership

"Divine love is a sacred flower which in its early
bud is happiness, and its full bloom is heaven."
                                        –Hervey

What is God, what is God's nature, where is God? Is It outside of me or is It within me? These are the questions that most of us ask ourselves from time to time. They are perfectly normal, because there is within each one an instinctive longing to understand and feel close to a Presence and a Power that is greater than oneself.

Looking at life as a whole, we sense a vast intelligence in action throughout the universe. We must conclude that there is a Power at work that the combined intelligence of man finds it difficult to imagine, let alone understand. For instance, what is the intelligence that created us an individual? What is the intelligence that causes our food to digest and our heart to beat? What is the force motivating the things that we do in the course of everyday living, such as expressing our feelings and emotions? These are phenomena that our intellect cannot fully explain on the basis of that which is observable. We find ourselves seeking to know more about that something which functions in and through all life, which we recognize to be much greater than our intellectual or ego-self. As individualized beings, we know that we are quite limited and must recognize that an intelligent something, greater than the combined intelligence of man, is active in this universe of ours. It is this something that we seek to understand. It is this something that humankind, throughout the ages, has designated as God in some form or another. Instinctively each is religious, for inwardly each senses the need to feel close to something greater than he or she is, greater than any friend or any group of friends.

Whatever the Intelligence that we call God is, being in and through all creation, It must be everywhere present. Therefore, we may conclude that God-essence is Infinite Presence and Infinite

13

Wisdom. If God is everywhere present, then God is not outside the self. God is one with us, and we are one with It. God, then, is everything that we are, the Power that creates us, the Power that animates us, the Intelligence within us, at all times guiding and directing every function of our lives. If we locate God as being everywhere, and therefore within the self, we must recognize that God is within all selves. With this understanding, we acquire the satisfying feeling that God is wherever we are, moving with us at all times. God is wherever we look, in all and through all creation. As we become aware of this, we are conscious of a Divine partnership with God and a warmer relationship with all whom we contact in the *business of living*.

We all express God in our own way. This self-expression, in its highest sense, is the giving of oneself in such a way that others may be helped and benefited. Human relationships represent the expression of God within us, unifying through communication with the expression of God in others. This is the meaning of our relationships and is the basis for all human associations and partnerships. In these relationships each contributes in some capacity to the well-being of others. This is so in all partnerships; each partner has something to contribute that the other lacks.

This is particularly true in the greatest and most wonderful of all partnerships, marriage. Each married partner, through giving of the self, contributes to the marriage relationship something that the other partner lacks. As this is recognized, there is a feeling on the part of each of the partners that the marriage state is good; it is beneficial; it is helpful. In this way, each partner in a good marriage relationship becomes a greater person, a more complete being. If this is realized and practiced by both husband and wife, happiness in marriage is assured.

As we think of a partnership with God, we recognize that this reciprocal-action principle of giving and receiving would also hold true. The Divine partner can supply us with that which we may lack and need at any given time. In turn, we increase our capacity as individualized beings to express more of the Divine potential in an objective and material way. This is the way in which God, the Absolute, expresses Itself in the relative world of conditions and affairs. "...my Father worketh hitherto, and I work." (John 5:7) Thus, each person becomes a partner and co-creator with the Divine, truly a *dispenser of the Divine gifts*.

As we come to understand God to be Infinite Love, Wisdom, and Power, we should learn to depend more and more upon God as our Divine partner and as the guiding influence in every department of our life. We should know that God will supply us with that bit of wisdom which we need in any situation of our everyday activities.

If we are honest with ourselves, we must admit that we are quite limited as far as our intellect is concerned. Any sense of frustration or self-condemnation arising from this realization is dispelled through our acceptance of a partnership with God. Have we not been told, "...I do nothing of myself; but as my Father hath taught me...." (John 8:28) also the promise, "...Son, thou art ever with me, and all that I have is thine" (Luke 15:31), becomes meaningful as we recognize and assume our Divine relationship with God, the universal wisdom and power. As we seek to embody this realization, we increasingly feel a closeness and a companionship that will respond to us with love and understanding according to our individual need. This response is much more effective than objective partnerships formed with individuals, for with God there can be no mistakes, false judgements, or erroneous actions,

We, as individuals, become more effective persons as we learn to depend on this wonderful Divine partnership. Our mental horizon is broadened; our sense of security and well-being is heightened. With this concept of God, we live a more complete life; our feeling of oneness with life and with each other becomes greater.

A happier life is experienced by those who feel that they may call upon this Presence within, as their Divine partner, to supply that which they need at any given time under any circumstance. This acceptance must be inwardly felt. God is a silent partner, never intruding when not asked to do so, but willing and able to assist at all times through any necessary objective channel, persons, situations, or experiences. For indeed God is in, through, and in Truth *is* all of these channels, persons, situations and experiences. As we turn to God, we are guided in all our endeavors through intuition and inspiration. Let us increasingly learn to depend on this Divine partnership. Let us embody the true meaning of the saying, "All things work together for good." (Rom. 8:28) Do we believe this is possible? We will never know because someone says it is so. We must put it to the test. Today is the time to begin to let our Divine partner assist us. The invitation must come from us.

TO SUM IT UP

Logic, reason, and intuition tells us that there is an intelligent Power behind, in, and through the universe and its activity.

The intelligent action of the Power creates and sustains the objective expressions of life.

We cannot conceive, with our intellect, all that God is or does.

Our thought leads us to the conclusion that God must be everywhere present (omnipresent); all wise (omniscient); all powerful to accomplish (omnipotent).

Being everywhere present, God is all that we are, expressing through us as us.

God is our partner, our life, our very being.

The intelligent action of God expresses harmony, balance, and beauty.

Love is the wisdom of God in action.

Our recognizing the nature of God and sensing our Divine partnership through our oneness with God paves the way for the *magic of love* to accomplish for us.

Greater happiness, self-expression, abundance, and peace of mind result as we increasingly feel the response of the Divine partner to our needs and desires for greater fulfillment in living.

4   The Law Of Freedom

> *"Love is the purification of the heart from self: it strengthens and enables the character: gives higher motive and nobler aim to every action of life."*
> *—Maria Jane Jewsbury*

It would appear to be a self-evident fact that we express freedom in our everyday living. We demonstrate freedom of choice every time we think. There is nothing that will step into our mind and say for us, "You cannot think," or, "You cannot choose." If this appears to happen, it is we, ourselves, who are saying it to ourselves. Outside sources may speak the words or may try to govern our thought, but this can never be done unless we, in effect, say, "I am going to let this person or situation influence my thinking." It may not be said in so many words, but the fact that we even *unconsciously* permit this influence in our thinking demonstrates the choice is ours.

What it is in our mental makeup that provides for and assures this *freedom of thought* is something that the philosopher, the religionist, and the creative thinker throughout the ages have been seeking to understand. Even though we may never know the complete answer, it is important for us to realize that as individuals, we do have this *power of choice* and that it has wisely been provided. It is a *built-in* aspect of our nature, and we will do well to accept this understanding and make it the basis for our future thinking and acting.

Our primary concern should be to use this *freedom to choose* in such a way as to bring into our lives a greater experience of those things which we call the "good things of life." This is a healthy attitude of mind. If we enjoy suffering or living a life of uncertainty or confusion, there is something radically wrong with our thinking. We are using our power of choice unwisely, limiting the very freedom that has been provided for us.

It has been said that Truth reveals Itself to us in a paradoxical form. This is also true of freedom. If we say there is a law of freedom, we are saying, in a sense, there is a bondage to freedom. This is because the law of anything is the way it operates and functions, and if we are to receive benefit from its action, there is a bondage to that particular law that requires adherence to the way it works. It is possible that our freedom, if not properly understood and used, may cause us to experience those hurtful, undesirable, and limiting aspects of living that we call bondage.

To illustrate how we can innocently and unknowingly misuse our freedom, the story is told of a man who had heard and accepted the fact that we are endowed with God-intended freedom of choice and, filled with enthusiasm, sought to put his new-found knowledge into practice at every opportunity. In talking to his wife, he said, "I have contacted a most wonderful philosophy, which says that we are free individuals with the ability to think and to choose. And," he continued, "I have made up my mind that you are to express your Divine individuality and, by golly, I'm going to see that you do!" This demonstrates how subtle the idea of freedom and bondage can be. In one breath this man is announcing freedom for his wife and in the next breath he is going to exercise his prerogative of freedom to force her to express herself a certain way. Well, we can draw our conclusions as to what will happen.

Another illustration of how a misunderstanding and misuse of the law of freedom can culminate in a disastrous result to all concerned is the case of Mr. A and Mr. B. Mr. A had been told that he was a Divine Being, empowered with the ability to think, choose, and express freedom of choice. As happens many times, he had listened but had heard only what he wanted to hear. Going down the street with his newly found knowledge uppermost in his mind, he met Mr. B, with whom he had had many an argument in the past. There was mutual distrust and dislike between the two. Mr. A thought to himself, "Here is my opportunity to exercise my God-intended freedom," and instead of passing Mr. B, he stopped in front of him and planted his fist forcefully and firmly on his nose. The object of Mr. A's "free expression" staggered around and finally straightening up, asked, "Why in the world did you do that!?"

"Well," said Mr. A, "I believe that each of us is a Divine individual who has a right to express his freedom of choice, and I was just exercising mine." With a confused but determined look on his face, Mr. B drew back his fist and sent a blow to the chin of Mr. A, knocking him out cold. Regaining consciousness, Mr. A looked up at Mr. B and asked, "What did you do that for?"

"That," said Mr. B, "was just to remind you that your freedom leaves off where my nose begins." Here is another example, facetious, of course, but one that could very well happen, of how we can misunderstand this idea of freedom.

Yes, through misunderstanding, we can unwisely use the law of freedom and thereby bind ourself to certain situations and inharmonious experiences that will be anything but pleasant.

We have ample proof in our everyday life that freedom or liberty of action does not mean license and that vigilance over one's thought and feeling is always a key to maintaining a life and experience that is desirable. A misuse of the so-called law of freedom can definitely result in bondage in our lives. We who use our feelings and imaginations in a way that does not go beyond our self-centered pride within ourselves and our own egocentric accomplishments are binding ourselves definitely to our own little world of limited experience. Through pride and, perhaps, arrogance, we are not willing to admit the need of others in our lives and refuse to accept the loving help that is offered where and when it is needed, which would add so much to our well-being.

As an example, let us suppose that someone came up to us and said, "Here is two thousand dollars. I no longer have any need for it, I want you to take it." Our reaction might be quite astounding and revealing. Our first thought might be, "What does this man have to sell; what is he trying to put over; what is he trying to get out of me?" The "doubting Thomas" would enter. In some instances our reaction might be, "Who does this man think he is, to give me this amount of money? Doesn't he think I can earn my own way? Why should I accept this good from him; I am not an object of charity." In such seemingly harmless ways we can exercise our freedom of choice to keep our good from us and to maintain bondage where there should be increased freedom.

This attitude of false pride that "I—the big I—shall do it and I shall accept no help from another" will keep us from communicating with those who may want to feel close to us. A feeling of closeness with others through communication by thought, word, and deed is so necessary to a happy, full life, but it can be shut off by an unwise use of freedom of choice. As individuals we have a right to think either well or harshly of people. It is our choice. We are acting unwisely, however, if we exercise this freedom by hating someone whom we feel has treated us unfairly or unjustly. The subject of our hatred is a source of bondage to us. It is not that someone else is *consciously binding* us in any way but rather that we *are binding ourselves* by dwelling on our hurts, imaginary or otherwise. Through hatred we frustrate that something within us which goes out to life and welcomes back from life the ideas, companionship, and love of others.

Jealousy, too, is a source of bondage, because it limits our possibility for an increased expression of good. If we are jealous of another's good we are in reality giving our attention to and emphasizing our own limitation. Using the law of life as the law of freedom, if we continue to dwell on some feeling of lack within ourselves, we give it power to bind us to our little round of everyday limitations.

Condemnation in any form is also a matter of exercising our freedom of choice. Every time we condemn another or ourselves, we are giving our attention to the less desirable and thereby limiting the possibility of greater good moving into our thinking and into our experience.

But, we may ask ourselves, if all this is true, what shall be our standard of procedure? What basis or yardstick can we employ in our thinking to assure us that our use of this law of freedom will not result in hurtful bondage? We have discussed a basic law of love, which we have likened to the Law of God. Therefore, if in our use of this Divine prerogative of freedom of choice, we seek to pattern our thoughts after what the Divine nature must be, we will be complying with the basic law of love. As we remove the frustrations and resistances to life from our thinking through love and understanding, we come to realize that our divine heritage and birthright, *freedom, is bound only by love*. Who could possibly object to the bondage of genuine love? *Even God is bound by Its divine nature.* Could humankind expect anything other than this? That which we understand we do not needlessly fear. When fear, with its fellow travelers of hatred, jealousy, suspicion, etc., is removed, only love can remain. Love is understanding, and understanding is the key to a harmonious use of the law of freedom. For instance, to the degree that we sense ourself, our real self, to be a Divine individual, we are free from any sense of condemnation, imagined or otherwise. Who could justly curse or condemn God or things of God? This inner feeling would release the forces of life, God-life, within us, because the moment the self-condemnation goes, there is the warmth and glow of self-approval based on understanding and love. Thus the way is paved for the freedom of action of the Life Principle and the Divine Presence within. Every time we can inwardly feel this Presence of Life moving freely, we are setting the stage for the establishment and maintenance of a helpful and happy expression of life.

As we come to understand others and think about them in terms of Divine beings expressing God-life, we free ourselves from the possibility of hurt from any source. We shall not be jealous of another person, nor shall we envy them as we come to truly understand them. Should there appear to be an attitude of misunderstanding or hurt in our relations with others, we should quickly bless and free them in love and understanding. This attitude of love and blessing is "agreeing with our adversary quickly." In this way we permit the magic law of love to have its way in our relationship with others.

As we consciously use the law of freedom with an increased understanding of what God must be like, as we know God is Love and see the Divine expressing in and through all nature, we establish within ourselves a feeling of strength and courage that only love can give to us. We free ourselves from a sense of separation from life. Faith is generated through the *will to believe* that God-Presence and Power is within us, and as we turn to It in understanding and love, so does It respond to us with an inner warmth and glow of certainty and security. Yes, there is a law of freedom at work in this life of ours, and we are using it every time we think and choose and react to life. Our highest and most productive use of our freedom should embody the realization that in and through all life flows the basic law of love, which is the infinite, eternal, and abiding Law of God. Knowing this, we will be perfectly willing to be bound by this abiding love and feel completely free to express ourselves fully, joyfully, and enthusiastically under that bondage. Using this yardstick to govern our use of the law of freedom, we shall find the response from life to be not of bondage or of hurt, but of love. We shall increasingly be aware, deeply within the self, of the presence of harmony, of vitality, and of strength, silently awaiting our discovery, recognition, and use in the course of our everyday living. We shall say to ourselves and to others, "It is true that I recognize and shall express my Divine birthright of freedom, but I shall know that as I do, I shall always be motivated by love and understanding. I shall be supported in all my endeavors by a sense of security and wholeness based on life's underlying principle of love." In this way and through this awareness, greater good increasingly moves into our thinking and acceptance of life. So shall the rich rewards of our freedom, wisely accepted and wisely administered, come into our lives. How will we use the law of freedom? The stakes are high. The rewards are satisfying. It's worth a try. This day—right now—we are free to choose, and choose we must. Let us resolve that understanding love shall govern our thought and desire in all of our choosing.

TO SUM IT UP

It is self-evident that we express freedom in living.

Self-awareness is the instrument of choice—choice is a thing of thought.

We cannot live another's life, nor can we *actually* choose or think for another.

Perhaps we shall never know *why* or *how* we have the power of conscious choice. This need not deter us from using this power of freedom in an affirmative and constructive manner.

The law of freedom is the principle involved in our use of our power of choice.

The law of freedom is bound by the law of love. It is never a license to hurt oneself or another.

A misuse or a mistaken use of freedom results in hurtful experiences or bondage. This is true of the misuse of any law of nature.

The yardstick for one's use of the law of freedom should be:
1. Does it embody right action for all concerned? If not, find another choice.
2. Does it embody thoughts of malice, hatred, jealousy, envy, condemnation, etc.? If so, get some new, affirmative thoughts and ideas working for the law of freedom to use.
3. Does it embody ideas of love, kindness, wisdom, thought-fullness of others, and God-good to the self? If it does, give it everything you've got with acceptance and faith—the Law will do the rest.

5 The Power of An Unfolding Consciousness

"Love is the fulfilling of the Law."

–Romans 13:10

ou are not the same person in many ways that you were "back there when." As we view ourselves and that which we are doing at this present period in our lives, no doubt we will conclude that the present picture is entirely different from that which we remember at some past point in our experience. Our reactions to life are not the same. We are not doing the same things. We have different types of associates and friends. In fact, we are quite different persons from the ones we were back there somewhere in those past years. Likewise, as we observe friends with whom we have associated over the years, we see that they also are different from the way they used to be. Something has changed. This change that has taken place in our life or in that of our friend, may be a happier, more desirable change. It may also be that, in some instances, it has not been a happy or satisfactory one.

Observations such as these stimulate certain questions. Why does this change happen? Why is it that we can apparently be an entirely different individual, for better or for worse, from the one we were some ten, twelve, twenty or more years ago? There must be a definite reason for it. Could we understand this reason or the process through which these changes take place, perhaps we could do something that would assure that present and future changes would be desirable.

We hear a great deal these days about states of consciousness. What about this idea of consciousness? Let's assume consciousness to mean one's mental awareness. *That of which one is mentally aware is one's individual state of consciousness.* We have said that through the *magic of the law of love* in action, one's mental awareness activates some force in nature, or God, causing certain things to happen in the life of the individual. Therefore, our state of consciousness or mental awareness is a determining factor in our use of this law of love to insure a harmonious and constructive expression of life.

Mental awareness does not necessarily mean that we are always *consciously* conscious of that which we are aware. To use an illustration, we are consciously conscious, if we remind ourselves to be so, of the fact that our heart is beating. We can hear it, observe it, and feel it. In a like manner, we can observe that the circulatory system is functioning. We are, however, unconsciously conscious that this is happening at all times. Below the surface of our conscious thinking there is an *unconscious awareness* (an aspect of consciousness) that is always with us.

We often see a little child mimicking an older person. The son will walk with his shoulders thrown back, arms swinging, and stepping along, following in the footsteps of his father. The daughter may be imitating certain actions of her mother. She will comb her hair, touch up with imaginary lipstick, or pretend she is doing the dusting. These are primarily unconscious actions on the part of the youngster. They are, however, acts establishing thought patterns that may later be consciously used.

Much of that which has happened to us in the past as well as that which is happening to us now, was then, or is now, an unconscious acceptance of something going on around us. This unconscious acceptance of things began at a very early age and is going on in each of our lives at the present moment.

Most of that which we have in the past accepted has long since been forgotten as a conscious remembrance. This, however, does not mean that its effect has been eliminated. Many of the things that we do in the ordinary routine of our day, such as the way we carry ourselves when we walk, how we generally react to life, or certain dominant mental attitudes, are based largely upon that which we have either *consciously* or *unconsciously accepted* over a period of time. In this way we find that our mental awareness, or consciousness, as we call it, is both conscious and unconscious at any given moment. This unfolding or growing awareness is taking place constantly in each of us. Our conscious thought influences our future thought acceptances and designates what type and to what extent past or unconscious thoughts will affect us. Knowing this, we can understand *why* we are in many ways entirely different persons now than we were ten or fifteen years ago. As we seek to let the law of love increasingly express in our life, it is helpful to know that this consciousness, or mental awareness, is never static. It is constantly changing according to our acceptance or belief about that which we observe, experience, or feel about things in general. The idea of belief is the key word; "according to our belief is it done unto us." According to the way we react *to* life do we experience *from* life. The source of one's beliefs has many facets. We would not deny, for instance, that there is a definite influencing power that we call race belief. We, as individuals, in the "being born" process, are subject to a tendency to accept unconsciously the beliefs of the human race at that particular time. This is as it should be. Otherwise we would be as isolated beings lost on the sea of life. Different countries, different races of people, have different characteristics. As individuals these beliefs and characteristics relative to the geographical location in which we are born become a part of our mental awareness. We do not deny this. It would be illogical to do so, for this is evidence of the Law of Cause and Effect in action.

In considering our mental awareness, we must also take into consideration *inherited tendencies* as one of its facets. The consciousness of our family, our immediate and remote ancestors, play a definite part in the early stages of our self-awareness. *Environment*, past and present, is a powerful determining factor in our mental awareness. We should realize, however, that these influencing factors need not necessarily continue to dominate our life, if to do so would be detrimental to our well-being. Once we consciously realize that certain conditions or states of mind (awareness) affect our experience, we have acquired the means for changing the effect of any previous condition or cause. To be consciously aware means self-awareness. To be self-aware means to be aware of the power of choice. Through this power of choice, we can release the power of love (God-Law) by giving our attention (conscious awareness) to something desirable and uplifting rather than the less desirable and limiting, regardless of its source or how long it has existed.

Self-awareness in humankind is something that does not just happen instantly or by chance but is a matter of unfoldment. Perhaps only God in God's Infinite Love and Wisdom knows why our souls have from the great soul-side of life pushed up through the influences of race belief—belief of ancestors, immediate family, inherited tendencies, and environment—and awakened to individual self-awareness. At that first moment of self-awareness we begin, through the power of choice (selection), to accept that which we feel to be true, regardless of past experience or any previous influence. Throughout our life this is a continuing, unfolding process of the potential of mind within us.

If our unfolding or growing consciousness is to bring greater good, more harmony, and richer expression of love into our experience, certain mental attitudes are important. Our reaction to those things which have happened in the past, that are happening now, and how we feel about that which is going to take place in the future, may have to be changed. As Paul said (I Cor. 13:11), "When I was a child, I spake as a child, I understood as a child, I thought as a child. But when I became a man, I put away childish things." *Maturity*, through an understanding self-awareness, takes away the power of consciously or unconsciously accepted less desirable beliefs, for it reveals them in their true perspective.

Faith is vitally important in changing seemingly fixed beliefs and bringing greater good into our experience. "Faith in what?" we may ask. Faith in the future. Faith in the here and now. William James described faith as "the will to believe." In the Bible we find, "there is a spirit in man and the inspiration of the Almighty giveth them understanding." (Job 32:8) Understanding is the key that opens the door to fuller acceptance of faith. We put this *understanding faith* to work by knowing that through the power of our unfolding consciousness, conditions, circumstances and experience will change. Just as our present experience may be entirely different from that of ten years ago, it follows that our present experience can change through the same power, as a result of our unfolding consciousness. The question for our consideration is what form this change of experience takes. It is at this point that our self-awareness of our power to choose is the determining factor.

If we have been anxious in our thinking, if we have harbored a sense of loneliness or separation from life, if we have always felt inadequate, our awareness of the presence of "spirit in man...which giveth him understanding" will be limited as will its givingness through us.

Our faculty of self-awareness enables us to see the truth about certain attitudes of mind, past and present, that are nourishing present undesirable conditions. As we search diligently and honestly for this truth, we find "the spirit in man...which giveth him understanding" reveals itself to us, through us, as our own self-awareness. As we feel our oneness with spirit, it becomes increasingly clear that there could not be two basic or infinite powers and that it must be the same Presence and Power that is in, through, and behind all things. This understanding is the "still small voice" within each, insisting that consciousness must unfold to ever greater heights of awareness.

The *magic of love* works through us as we consciously open our awareness to it. The solution to our limited concepts, beliefs, and experiences is largely a matter of letting go of the disbeliefs, the less desirable beliefs, the anxieties, and the uncertainties. The conclusion or "will to believe" that there is a Wisdom and an Understanding within each of us at *this moment* that knows how to bring about everything necessary to establish a greater good in our life, is setting the law of love in action. With this understanding faith, a greater feeling of belonging will be ours. These affirmative attitudes will grow out of the ashes of the less desirable mental states of awareness, regardless of how they came into being or what caused them, as our new awareness built on faith and understanding that the past influences or future anxieties have only as much power as we give them. Our *dominion* over our experiences results from our self-awareness of the presence of God-Spirit in us, as us, ever spiraling upward through us as our unfolding consciousness.

Perhaps we shall never know completely what the Infinite Presence is in its entirety, nor shall we know the full significance of the tremendous capacity that we have within ourselves at any time to use the great law of love. As we deeply feel this Presence within ourselves, however, we become aware that harmony, beauty, and those things that we call the "good things" of life are basically God-like. We sense that God is in and through all things and those things that we need to make life more expressive, the happiness that comes from friendship and the unfettered expression of life, all of these and more are our Divine birthright.

This awareness is the power of an unfolding consciousness that assures us that in faith, belief, and acceptance, we can say, "Through the *magic of love* as the action of God, I am deeply aware, as I turn within at any given moment, of this Presence as peace of mind 'which passeth understanding.'" We must be patient and persistent. Unfoldment is a growing process. Our state of awareness at this moment moves us to that person we will be when we look back at any time and say, "I am not, in many ways, the same as I was back there when."

TO SUM IT UP

Change in one's mental, emotional, and environmental makeup is normal and natural. You are not now the same person in many ways you were at any given point in your past experience.

Our mental awareness is our state of mind, both conscious and subjective (unconscious), at any given time.

Our mental awareness changes as the result of our reaction to our experience, thought, and inner feeling about ourselves and life in general.

The subjective aspect of one's mental awareness includes early childhood experiences, environmental situations (past and present), inherited tendencies, and so-called "race belief" or the "collective unconscious" of Dr. Carl Jung.

Mental awareness is the governing factor in our present and future state of being, both mental and environmental.

God in his wisdom and love has endowed us with self-awareness.

To the degree that we use self-choice wisely, intelligently and with love, we become mature in our thinking and our actions.

Growth is normal. Mature, satisfying, and productive growth follows an increased awareness of love, beauty, and balance as the basic, essential goodness in and through all life.

It is done to us according to our belief.

6   Agree with Thine Adversary

"For love is but the heart's immortal thirst—
To be completely known and all forgiven."
                               –Henry Van Dyke

"Just keep traveling in the direction you are going and you will arrive at the corner you just left." If you were walking down the street and someone said this to you, you would be justified in thinking that the person didn't know what they were talking about. And, of course, you would be correct, because no one can travel in opposite directions at the same time. Although not quite as obvious, it would be just as impossible a situation if someone said to you, "Just keep on hating this individual long enough and you will come to love him." It is illogical to suppose that one can, mentally, go in two diametrically opposed directions at the same time.

Obviously if we are to return to the corner of the street that we have just left, we will have to reverse our direction and start walking back to that corner. It is just as obvious that if we are going to love another person, any attitude of hatred that may be in our mind toward that person will have to be eliminated through some means or method.

We have been told to *agree with our adversary and he will flee from us.* This is good advice, both philosophically and psychologically, when practiced in the proper manner. It would be logical, in "agreeing with our adversary," that we would have to come to a place in our thinking where the idea of having an adversary, someone or something to fight, would have to be changed. Perhaps there is no more unhappy person in the world than one who feels that life is against him. Such a person will feel that he is separate and apart from life, that he has to fight for all that he acquires. He will probably be convinced that people do not like him and that life is just one struggle after another. People who accept this inner conviction finds that life gives back to them that which they feel within their own mind. They will find these ideas of hostility, separation, and duality reflected back to them by people in their environment. They are very liable to find that things are made difficult for them as they move through life. Only unhappiness, a sense of frustration, and futility can result from a sustained feeling that life is against us.

No one actually wants to have unhappy experiences or to live *an unfulfilled life*. The problem, however, is always how to change the direction of our thinking and reaction to life in such a way that the apparent antagonism, or the feeling that we are constantly confronted by adversaries, will be eliminated. The necessary change of direction in our thinking is never accomplished by ignoring the undesirable facts or experiences. On the other hand, the situation is not changed by continually asserting, "I have an adversary in every direction with whom I must contend."

Using the example of "getting back to the corner which we have just left," no good purpose would be accomplished by arguing with the person who says, "We must keep on going in the direction in which we are going in order to arrive back at that corner." Argument would only set up the basis for contention within his thought and within our mind emphasize the feeling that we have an adversary to overcome. The easiest, most harmonious and productive way to handle such a situation would be to agree, even though silently, with such an individual. We can let him have his own opinion, while inwardly maintaining our ideas founded on logic and reason. Following our own conviction, we would simply turn around and go back toward the corner we just left. Thus no one would be hurt, and no one would have to "save face."

The same analogy would hold true regarding our desire to turn hatred and malice into love. Our reaction to the one who said if we would just keep on hating this individual long enough, we would come to the place where we could love him, would be that this person is mistaken—and they have a right to be mistaken, if they so wish. Should we enter into verbal contention with him, however, the result would only be confusion. Probably nothing would be accomplished, and we would find that actually we had created an adversary with whom we must contend.

In these situations, the solution would be to seek and find a *basis of agreement with that which seems to be the adversary*. Such a point of agreement with people who tell us we should keep on going in the same direction would be that they have a right to their opinion and belief. Each of us agrees that we must *keep on traveling to arrive at our desired destination*; however, within our mind we would know it would not be in the direction that a particular person had told us we must go.

In the case of love and hate, we would both agree that these are both powerful emotions. The one who says we must hate in order to love may think that he is giving us good advice. We give him that privilege. The point of agreement would be that feeling and emotion are involved. But in our particular opinion it would be a different type of emotion from that of hate that would lead to love.

In both these instances there existed a *duality of thought and opinion*. In both instances, we found that we could probe behind the apparent duality and find a basis for agreement. It is obvious that any process that is going to eliminate the feeling of having an adversary will have to begin with some such *basic point of mutual agreement*.

Could we not apply this reasoning to those things which we consider our adversaries in everyday experiences? Those adversaries nurtured by a subtle belief in basic duality are the problems of sickness as opposed to health, abundance as opposed to lack, friendship as opposed to hatred and opposition on the part of others. These and many other apparent opposites are those things which interfere with productive, harmonious, and happy living.

The most effective way to counteract these apparent dualities of experience is not to *run away or ignore them*. If we view them with an understanding mind and heart, knowing that they are not illusions but actual experiences through which we go, we are taking the first step in agreeing with our adversary. For instance, if we supposed that abundance resulted from one power and poverty from another, we would have to agree that while such appeared to be the case, in reality this could not possibly be true, or there would be a basic duality of power in the universe. The point of agreement in arriving at this conclusion would be the realization that in either case, limitation or abundance represents some degree of this world's material good. Poverty or lack cease to be thought of as the product of a *power of limitation*, but would simply be a limited experience of substance that could very well be an experience of abundance under the proper, or different, circumstances. This agreement alone would mean that a basis would be provided for "a ceasing to struggle" against an unseen adversary. This "loose him and let him go" attitude would tend to relieve the very pressure and mental tension that in itself could keep one from experiencing more abundant living. We have been told that we cannot serve God and mammon. This statement seems to be declaring that there is God or Spirit as opposed to mammon, or material things. Seeking to follow this admonition has been the source of great unhappiness in many lives. Each of us has within us an innate desire to so express ourself in such a way as to experience those things that are harmonious, lovely, beautiful, and productive. In light of the apparently opposing powers of God and mammon, one's thought logically would be, "I do enjoy the good things of life, the material things make life so enjoyable. But on the other hand, I do not want to do anything that will antagonize God." Unless the apparent adversary of mammon as opposed to God (good) is resolved, the idea of duality and its accompanying desire to go two ways at the same time will lead to frustration, confusion, and their resulting ills and hurts. If this is to be avoided, there is a definite need to agree with that which seems to be our adversary.

This would call for a common meeting ground where we could agree with the statement in such a way as to allow others to have their interpretation of it but at the same time insist that we also have the privilege of our interpretation. We can say to ourselves, "Of course, I cannot serve God and mammon because, in my estimation, that which I call mammon cannot be separated from that which I call God." The objective world of material things designated as mammon are outward expressions of God. They are God-ideas in form. Once we have agreed that material things are God substance in form, the thought of opposing powers would be eliminated and automatically the tension accompanying such belief in duality would be removed from our minds. This will entirely change our reaction to the statement that we cannot serve God and mammon. By agreeing with our adversary, it disappears. This is not God *and* mammon. There is only God expressing *as* mammon. We are often concerned as some particular good thing or experience changes our life. Even the thought of change often becomes our adversary. *We have built our security on certain things.* Again, we must agree with our adversary. *Change is normal.* True security is not based primarily on objective things or situations, but on an inner realization that God substance is limitless as are God ideas and that, as a God-individual, we have access to both at all times. With this understanding, material things would cease to be something to be struggled for, to be struggled with, or to be hoarded away as something that will give us power in our life and all too often over the lives of others. By looking at and through any given situation where there seems to be an adversary and finding a basis for agreement, we open our minds to the miracle of love to do its work. As the contention in our innermost thinking is removed, we will find that life will become much more worthwhile, and through the law of attraction, any apparent contention on the part of others toward us in our everyday relationships will be removed. As this miracle of understanding love goes to work, there will be no desire for good for ourselves at the expense of another or that would not be possible for another to experience, should they so desire.

In any confused or unpleasant situation, it is always well to surround the other person involved, as well as ourselves, with a feeling of love and understanding. *It takes two to cause a disagreement,* just as it takes a basic belief in duality to cause much of the unhappiness, uncertainty, and insecurity that we experience in living. Once we can feel our oneness with the Infinite Presence of God as Love and come to realize it is the motivating force in and through all life and all persons, we have the basis for agreeing with any apparent adversary.

The miracle of love awaits only the removal from our minds of the necessity of the apparent obstructions or contentions, disagreement, and belief in duality to bring into our life happiness, peace of mind, and contentment in our relationships with others. The beauty of it all is that we do not have to *make* it happen. It happens if and as we *let* it happen. Light will banish darkness—affirmation dethrones negation—water reaches its own level by its own weight. We do not *have* to *make* any of this happen. Once we have initiated the action, the results are automatic.

How do we let the miracle of love take place? In agreement with our adversaries, real or imaginary, lies the answer. Love is the common denominator that not only provides the basis for agreement but evokes a response after its own nature in any situation. Watch the response to love in the newborn baby. Observe the reaction of anyone toward whom understanding love is directed. Watch violent disagreement, hatred, or seeking to hurt quickly fade into nothingness as it is met by the warmth of understanding love. Wild animals, domestic pets, and even plants respond definitely to thoughts of love and blessing. Too good to be true? *Nothing is too good to be true.* Try it conscientiously and consistently. "With God all things are possible." God has no adversaries. God is love and "Love is the lodestone of life."

TO SUM IT UP

No one can, physically, go in two opposite directions at the same time. It is just as illogical to say that one can mentally accept two ideas that contradict each other at the same time.

We cannot *agree with our adversary* on any point of contest as long as we feel that we have an adversary. A change in one's thinking *about the adversary* is necessary and is the *basis* for agreement.

Much of the unhappiness humankind experiences is caused by a belief that life is against us and that we are beset by many adversaries. Finding a basis for agreement with life or any apparent adversary eases the situation.

To think that we can serve God and mammon is to believe in *basic duality*. As we understand that the *objective world is God in manifestation*, the adversary of a belief in two basic powers (duality) is eliminated.

Many times we fight changes in our life, situations, friends, experiences, or ideas. This apparent adversary (fear of change) is eliminated as we agree that change is normal in one's expression of life.

Love (understanding) is the common denominator running through all life and is the *basis for a meeting of the minds* in our relationship with others. Understanding (love) is the point of agreement that enables us to agree with our adversaries and cause them to "flee from us" as a power to hurt.

7   *Love Your Way To Health*

"It is the duty of men to love even those who injure them."

–Marcus Aurelius Antoninus

What is the most precious gift that could be given to you? No doubt your answer would be the gift of perfect health, for good health assures us of so many of the worthwhile and gratifying experiences in living. Yes, it is good to be able to say, "I feel wonderful!" With modern research in the fields of science, medicine, psychiatry, psychology, and religion we find, however, that to truly say, "I feel wonderful" depends on more than the so-called physical state of our body. It is now demonstrated that *our body responds constantly to our attitude of mind,* how we think during the day, how we feel about ourself, about situations and about others. No longer can we draw a definite line and say, "This aspect of my being is my body, this is my mind, and still another aspect is my soul."

Naturally, when we are enjoying health we are enjoying a general feeling of ease, not only ease of the body but ease of mind. Good health, then, could be described as that feeling we have when no part or aspect of our body is calling its attention to us in any way because it is functioning in an easy, harmonious manner. If one is conscious of strain, tension, irritation, or inflammation, or any of those discomforts which most of us experience at times, we would say, "Here is evidence of a state of ill health or disease as opposed to a state of health or ease." These two situations provide the basis for saying, "I feel wonderful!" or, "I don't feel well."

In seeking to change a state of disease to one of ease, regardless of what method we use, *it will be helpful to think of health of body as being a perfectly natural and normal state.* This natural and normal state is one where all bodily functions are harmonious, in that all actions throughout the body are taking place in a perfectly balanced, cooperative

35

manner. This would mean that every organ, every gland, every nerve, every muscle, and every other aspect of the body would be doing the job it is supposed to do in connection with the overall body function. It would mean that there would be perfect cooperation and harmony of action among the organs, the glands, the nerves, and all the other functions of the body, whether they be circulatory or those involved in the processes of assimilation and elimination.

As we consider these aspects of good health, we recognize that these ideas are almost identical to those which we have designated as the *qualities of love*; i.e., *harmony, beauty, balance, self-giving, etc.* Within the last few years many books such as *Love or Perish* and *Love Against Hate* have been written, emphasizing the importance of love in relation to man's mental and physical well-being. *Love does have the power to work apparent miracles in every aspect of our living.* If we love life, we are viewing life with a wise and mature, yet trusting attitude of mind. Through the eyes of love, we have the ability to look through seeming uncertainties and insecurities of experience and acquire the larger vision of a *basic state of integrity* in, through, and behind all things. This basic integrity we have called God, Nature, or the Life Principle itself. With the eyes of love, we have the ability to look at and through the seeming unpleasantness that may be experienced from time to time in our relationships with others. We learn to see the real, basic person involved in all of our human relationships. We have the ability to love people even though we do not like some of the things they may do. To the degree that we consciously develop this insight leading to the ability to love in spite of appearances, do we eliminate frustration, anxiety, hatred, and other fears and reap the reward of "good feeling" or "feeling good," which is so necessary to good health.

In thinking about ourselves and our relationship to life, an attitude of understanding love enables us to look through and behind certain aspects of our own makeup and certain of our actions toward others that perhaps would not have our highest approval. This is not denying appearances but is making use of an instrumentality that will elevate our awareness in such a way as to understand that we, as well as others involved, are Divine beings in spite of objective appearances.

If perfect health is the normal harmony and balance of all the bodily functions, anything that disrupts, frustrates, or interferes with this balanced expression would result in ill health or disease. If one's mind is cluttered with feelings of hatred, malice, envy, jealousy, or any mental attitude that is the opposite of the feeling of love, one is sowing seeds that may well cause disease in his or her experience. Mental irritation, from whatever source, causes certain glandular and bodily functions to become over- or underactive. For instance, where one is filled with anxiety, uncertainty, or insecurity, the feeling of tension results in a type of stress that definitely affects certain glandular activity. We know that sustained mental attitudes of confusion can definitely cause various types of headaches and is thought to be, in a great many instances, the underlying cause of congestions resulting in the "common cold" and similar congested bodily afflictions.

It is not difficult for us to see that negative or unhappy attitudes of mind may interfere with the harmonious and normal activity of health. If this is so, then it would be reasonable to assume that harmonious, peaceful, happy, and understanding attitudes of mind would be important factors in removing obstructions to the normal flow of life and again establishing health as one's experience. These affirmative attitudes of mind are the qualities of love itself. Again, we see the way in which the *miracle of love* may bring a state of health into one's life that, it would seem, is not only normal and natural but is in essence the very Nature of God expressing in and through His creation.

But, we may ask, "How are we going to raise our level of awareness or feeling from those less desirable attitudes of mind in order to embrace the affirmative and constructive attitudes of love?" This is not always an easy thing to do. For each of us, however, there would seem to be only one place to begin to do it and that is *within our thinking and inner feeling* about things. This is our state of awareness. God has given us the necessary tools with which to work, the power to *think*, to *choose*, to *imagine and to feel*. The only time we can begin to consciously use these tools constructively and for definite purposes is right *now* at this moment. None of us can actually live in the past or in the future. "Now is the appointed time." Now is the time to begin to practice those affirmative attitudes of mind that are so beneficial. Be persistent. Be courageous. Be understanding, calm, and considerate of the self and others. *Persistency in itself is an affirmative attitude when the desire is constructive.*

It will be helpful to again and again remind ourselves that through the ages love has been used as a synonym for God. As we think thoughts embodying the nature of love, we are thinking God-like thoughts and therefore consciously cooperating with God-life. In this way we permit the wisdom of instinctive life to express through us normally as perfect health. The question may arise, "How can I consciously cooperate when I do not know very much about the physical makeup of my body—how do the organs and glands work, what motivates the various types of circulation and other bodily functions?" No one really knows all the answers to these whys and hows. It is reported that Edison's reply to the question, "What is electricity?" was, "Electricity is; use it." We have, it would seem, consciously very little to do with the bodily functions at the subjective level of action, except to disrupt their normal activity through unwise thoughts, feelings, and emotions. The wise and affirmative approach to health would be, "We did not create life nor do we sustain it. A power greater than we are is responsible for this life of ours."

As we acknowledge this God-life as our life, as we love it, bless it, and cooperate with it to the best of our ability, the whys and hows will not be too important. To paraphrase Edison's remark about electricity, "Life *is*—live it, use it, enjoy it, love it!" And, we may add, as with the case of electricity, the more we use it wisely, *according to its nature*, the more happy and productive will be the result.

As we think of God as Love, and Life as the expression of God, it becomes easy for us to accept that, even though we do not intellectually know *how* to make life function harmoniously as health, instinctive Life or God in action within us knows exactly what to do. Our conscious cooperation in maintaining a state of health would then become a matter of letting our thoughts and feelings embrace more and more of what the basic nature of life and God must be. Persistently dwelling on thoughts of love, wisdom, balance, beauty, courage, and harmony would be the means one would use for elevating one's awareness. It will help us to consistently entertain the attitudes of mind so necessary for health if we think of disease of body not as an entity of itself but rather an experience resulting from a limited or frustrated activity of the Divine action of life. Renewed health then could be said to be the logical result of mentally letting go of those inner feelings and attitudes of mind that have frustrated and confused, and turning our attention to those mental attitudes that would embody the aspects of love. These basic attitudes of harmony, beauty, balance, and joy would lead to feelings of security, confidence, courage, and a sense of well-being, which are the ingredients of emotional stasis.

Thinking of our body and its functions in this manner, we will cease trying to consciously, mentally manipulate, change, or run the various functions of the glands, organs, etc. We will have faith to believe that if we will but pattern our thoughts and feelings according to what the nature of God must be, that God, as instinctive life, will automatically do the rest. We will begin to think of our physical body as the expression of a Divine idea. A wonderful thing of beauty. Thoughts of condemnation or criticism of our body that may have been entertained in the past will be dissolved as we begin to praise our physical body. We will increasingly sense the effortless rhythm and harmony of all its various functions.

We should view this physical body with its organs, glands, nerves, tissue, bones, etc., as the manifestation of a Divine God-intended idea, which we did not create. It is God-created and God-sustained. In this way we will begin actually to cultivate an attitude of love regarding our body, enabling us to say and really mean, "This body is a wonderful and beautiful creation. I am grateful for it. I praise it. I love it."

Yes, there is a miracle of love, and you can use it to love your way to health.

TO SUM IT UP

Perfect health is our most precious possession.

Health is not confined to physical functions alone.

Our being is physical, mental, and spiritual. The balanced and harmonious action of each of these aspects of our makeup is essential to health.

Negative thoughts and emotions such as fear, frustration, and tension, interfere with normal bodily functions.

Affirmative thoughts and emotions permit normal bodily functions to express.

A person is conscious of ill health or disease when malfunction or maladjustment within the body makes itself felt.

We are conscious of a feeling of well-being or health when we are not conscious of bodily functions except as a feeling of ease.

Understanding love is the basis of all affirmative thoughts and emotions. Love is essential to good health.

Love in action is the magic that integrates the spiritual, mental, and physical aspects of our being.

Love in action follows a persistent effort to maintain an awareness of the affirmative attributes of love in all of our thinking. This practice in relation to ourself, our environment, and all of life is necessary to maintain health.

Health is normal and natural. It is natural and normal to love. Ill health is not normal and is a frustrated expression of life.

Through affirmative attitudes of mind, we can literally *love* our *way to health*.

8   You Are Greater Than You Think

"Love is love's reward."

–Dryden

Wouldn't it be an insurmountable task to consciously direct every aspect and activity of our life? Just suppose we had to consciously supervise the digesting of our food or the beating of our heart. What a task it would be to give directions to the nerves and muscles involved in taking a single step or to consciously control our diaphragm in order to breathe. It almost gives one a headache to think about it, and yet these are only a few of the hundreds of minute activities that are carried out by an *intelligent power within each of us.* We have stated the self-evident fact that we did not consciously create ourselves. This in itself is evidence that there is a power that did create us and that, as we have observed, sustains us. We are also aware that there is a Presence and Power that *has guided us* through many apparent difficulties.

Most of us have had times in our life when we seemed to have lost our way. We did not know the answer to some vital and pressing need. The props had been knocked out from under us, and we did not know where, or to whom, to turn for help. At such times one is forced, often through sheer desperation, to realize the presence of and call upon the power of something greater than *one's intellect* for help. Many seeming miracles have taken place through being forced to climb down from one's egotistic perch long enough to "let go and let God."

This Presence and Power that comes to our assistance has been described as that "Love that will not let us go." Why can we not only know more about this Presence and Power but increasingly come to depend on it? Why can we not invite it to constantly move wisely and lovingly in and through each and every need or desire that we may have? Why should we wait until we are at our wit's end or until we are forced, through sheer necessity, to open our minds and hearts to the "very present help" that awaits only our acceptance? The answer is that we can, and we do not have to wait. Right now, we can begin to do this by increasing our understanding that there is a Presence and Power within us that knows how and what to do and that, by increasing our faith or "will to believe," it will do it. We can know it is the same power and intelligence that makes us walk when we say or think, "I want to walk." It is the same love that takes care of our breathing and heartbeats that will guide us, effectively and affirmatively, in the many decisions that we are called upon to make from day to day.

With increased understanding and faith, we can know that even though we do not know all there is to know about everything, we can know that we know enough to realize that something within us does, and we can *learn to let it do it*. This state of awareness and acceptance is something that each of us has to accomplish, and we do this definitely and deliberately *through* practice. To be sure, it isn't always easy. If we have had a past history of negative, unhappy, or confused thinking, it is not easy for us to say and really accept that this is all done with; it is part of the past, and we will have no more to do with it. But this is exactly what we have to do. This is because we are dealing with a Presence and Power that will and must do our bidding. "It is the Father's good pleasure to give us of the Kingdom of God." The gift has been made. The acceptance becomes our decision.

Understanding faith comes with a persistent endeavor to view the experiences of living from the standpoint of unity and wholeness. As we have discussed previously, there could not be two Infinites or there would be chaos and not cosmos. If this is true, then there could not be two ultimate basic powers. Only one. One life, one power, one intelligence from which the multiplicity of forms and experiences originate and become the objective world in which we live.

The spiritual vision of the mystic is "the single eye" of the one who practices faith—looking at objective facts, conditions, and affairs, not as things of themselves but as objectifications of the One Presence and the One Power. God, then, is the Absolute, the First Cause, the All-in-All from which all things come. God is both *creator* and *created* and the sustainer of all things.

Did you ever wonder why you were born? It doesn't pay to try to figure this out, feeling we must know all the answers, for perhaps we shall never know the *why* of it. We can, however, know with certainty that we were born into this objective experience of living and that of necessity we must be expressions of the one Source, Reality, or God. We are divine beings, for we must partake of the Divine Nature.

As the poet said, "Thou has made us, thine we are. Our hearts are restless till they rest in Thee." The "resting in Thee" is the calm sense of assurance that comes from the deep realization of our oneness with God and life. As divine individuals, we are never *all* that God is at any time. All that we are, however, is *some aspect* of what God is all the time. Knowing this, we can say with assurance. "There is that within me which is greater than anything that has ever happened to me, seems to be happening to me now, or that I feel may happen to me in the future. It is that which created me and sustains me. It is something upon which I can depend."

That within us which enables us to say and know these things is our *self-awareness*, which, when *consciously directed*, becomes our power of choice. Power of choice is a human *must* for a Divine individual. By our use of this power we create our conditions and affairs. Through this power, which is our *use* of God-Power, each of us actually controls his destiny. "It is done unto us as we believe."

We have said that understanding faith comes with a persistent endeavor to view the experiences of living from the standpoint of unity and wholeness. This, as thinking beings, we can and must do if we are to change the less desirable experiences and to bring more of the *infinite potential* of God-good into our lives. To one who practices and diligently seeks "first the kingdom of God" or heaven, will come the conviction that the original, basic or first cause of all existence is one of unity—not duality. Such a one will have a new insight of TRUTH, which will sustain him and be the means of using the power within to actually eliminate the undesirable from his experience. He will know that experiences, as well as objective things, did not *create themselves* nor do they sustain themselves. They are created and sustained by the One Power. Through our use of this One Power, we create and sustain our experiences. We will know that any less desirable experience in our life has no power to sustain itself once that which supports it (acceptance), withdraws that support.

With this new insight, we will know that things truly are not always what they seem to be. We will view lack not as a power of lack expressing but rather as a limited acceptance of the infinite potential of substance and supply. We will view the emotions of envy, hatred, and malice and their logical results of frustration, unhappiness, and hurt, not as the action of an evil power, but rather as the way we are using the One Power. These so-called negative emotions have assumed a power they do not have. They exist as a result of one's almost complete lack of acceptance of love and understanding.

As one persistently practices the awareness of oneness, a belief in a power of sickness as opposed to a power of health cannot be accepted. Sickness or ill-health is seen as but a frustrated or limited expression of life as it should be expressing. We have somehow refused to accept our divine heritage and have permitted, either *consciously* or *unconsciously*, sickness to assume a power that it does not have. The answer to any illness would seem to lie in the removal of the frustrating or inhibiting cause, thus removing its support. Once this is done, its seeming power is removed and it can no longer exist.

No matter how much bondage, limitation or unhappiness we have experienced, our Divine nature and heritage provides the way for its elimination. We are *greater than we think*. But we, and we alone, must permit the greater potential to help us. It cannot do this effectively if we persist in thinking of our ourselves in terms of isolated beings. We must think of ourselves as being one with the one basic Power and Presence. To do this effectively, we cannot continue to believe in duality.

As we persist in our endeavor to "seek first the kingdom" and its rightness, to realize our own Divine heritage, we will develop the insight that enables us to sense the Divine in and through all creation. Our practice of this knowledge becomes the way in which we permit the affirmative creative power to influence our every thought and reaction to life. Thus we learn to walk hand in hand with the "Love that will not let us go," knowing that the Power and Presence that created us, by its very nature, must and will continue to sustain us in all phases of our living. The power is not in the intellect of humankind. The intellect directs and leads the mind to a place of acceptance. In realization and acceptance lies our power to live more effectively.

The gift has been made and our *greatness* lies in our *ability to accept*.

Note: For added inspiring ideas and insight into the hidden potential of humankind, the author recommends the works of Dr. Norman Vincent Peale, notably *The Power of Positive Thinking*.

TO SUM IT UP

We did not consciously create ourselves, therefore it is self-evident that there is a Power greater than our intellect that created us.

We do not consciously direct many of the essential bodily functions, therefore it is self-evident that there is a power and intelligence within us that directs all those bodily functions that sustain us in our expression of life.

Through understanding and faith we can come to depend on this power, greater than our intellect, for *guidance in all phases of living*.

As there could not be two Infinites, the power that sustains us and that we use must be some aspect of the Infinite Power, or God.

We are Divine beings, for all that we are must be some aspect of that which the Infinite, or God, is.

The basis for our dominion over our lives, conditions and affairs lies in our *recognition of our Divine origin* and our *power of choice*.

Spiritual insight enables us to know that God is in and through all things, and that *all things are expressions of God.*

The intellect has no power of its own to make things happen. It is important, however, in that it is the faculty that gives consent and permits the one Power to do our bidding.

Part Two

MEDITATIONS

*"If ye know these things
happy are ye if ye do them."*

–John 13:17

Introduction To Meditations

"Never self-possessed or prudent, love is all abandonment."

–Emerson

*U*p to this point we have endeavored to show that there is a vitality, effectiveness, and apparent "magic" in our basic powerful emotion of *love*—that in the use of this precious "gift of gifts" lies the key to untold splendors in one's life that challenge the *intellect* of humankind to completely comprehend. The gift has been made, the way has been shown, but it remains for each of us to open the doorway to the "imprisoned splendor." The law of love, as with all other laws of life, must be understood and definitely used in order to receive more of its potential good.

As we have pointed out, the law of mathematics remains simply a potential possibility unless it is understood. Through its *understanding* and *use*, new vistas and new opportunities are open to the mind and experience of each of us. This is also true of the laws of chemistry, physics, music, and all the basic laws of life that we have at our disposal. The law of love is no exception, for it would seem that love must be brought into action in using all of Nature's laws if we are to experience good through our understanding of these laws. Nor is it enough to say we must understand, for that is just one-half the story. We can understand the laws of mathematics perfectly in all its phases but, unless we *do something* about it, it will not add up a column of figures or provide the square root of a given number; it will continue to remain just what it is—a potential still to be tapped in order that it may demonstrate its ability to accomplish something definite for us. The same is true of the laws of chemistry, physics, and all other laws of life. They remain potential until, and unless, something is done with them.

As far as we are concerned, that something which is done is what we ourselves do about it. We can use our understanding of any law, put it to work, and it will respond to us. It gives up its apparent secrets and works *seeming miracles* in our lives. So it takes both understanding and use to receive the potential blessing resident within any law of life.

Even knowing this is not enough, for we must "begin to start" or nothing will happen. It will all be a *grand idea* and an *idle dream*, remaining a beautiful potential unless something is done about it. The doing becomes a matter of choice, and we have the power of choice. This choice can be made *right now*. We cannot make it any sooner, and to procrastinate only means to delay the benefits any law of nature is willing to give to us and *must* give to us as we deliberately tap its potential possibility.

The choice is an act of mind or thought. That which puts the choice in action is also a mental act, but it is somewhat different. Action denotes movement, and to begin to put a choice into action, one must begin to move mentally with the idea involved in the choice. This is more than an intellectual process, for it involves feeling and imagination. In using the law of music, let us suppose one sat at a piano, adjusted his music, and placed his hands on the keyboard, saying to himself, "I understand music, I can read the notes, I know the characters, now why does not music come forth?"

The answer is that we are not following through in our choice. We must begin to feel what it means to play the music. In our imagination, we must feel the harmony, beauty, and action potential within the law of music and symbolized on the printed page, moving in and through us as action. We must, in addition, know and sense that the musical instrument responds willingly to us. The same process is necessary in our definite use of any law. The sequence would be: first, an understanding of what we want to do and something of how it would happen (the law involved); second, we must make the choice (this is what we want to do and we are going to do it); third, we must unite the understanding and the choice with desire, imagination, and feeling (mentally image ourselves entering into the action of our choice and it becoming our experience). It is the imagination and feeling that gives vitality, fire and enthusiasm to our thoughts and desires. Without it, nothing much is accomplished. With it, the doorway to the storehouse of the great potential of life is ever widened. In this manner, each of us may provide the way for the bountifulness of Nature, or God, to pour its blessings through us in our everyday living. This may seem to be a *miracle* to us, but to God, or Nature, it is just an expression of the Law of Life—the Law of Love.

All of this process in the technique described may seem to be highly involved and to entail considerable effort on our part. It is true that the *effort* must be made to accomplish anything in this life, but it need *not* be one of strain or tension. In fact, we should seek to avoid strain, for that, in a sense, will defeat our purpose. We should always bear in mind that any law will work for us by its own effort if we provide the way for it to work.

The ideas we have been talking about up to this point deal with *how* we may provide this way in order for something to take place in our experience. There are many mental approaches that we may use to pave the way for the Basic Law of Life to move effectively through ourself. Each would embody the three steps mentioned above: understanding, choice, and feeling and imagination. The ancients practiced rituals, special incantations, and various forms of supplication—all effective to a certain extent. In more modern times, in addition to prayer in some form, we have psychoanalysis, psychosomatic medicine, autosuggestion or autoconditioning, as ways of using the power of mind for specific therapeutic purposes.

Affirmative prayer and meditation, separately or in combination, prove most effective in the process of opening our minds and hearts to let the law of life accomplish through us. Affirmative prayer is not *doubtful petition*, nor is affirmative meditation *idle wishing or daydreaming*. In one's use of prayer and meditation, definite ideas would be involved. For instance, meditation is for the purpose of giving one's attention *to* an idea, thus taking our attention *from* other ideas for a definite period of time. In a sense it could be likened to concentration, except that meditation does not embody strenuous effort. It is not a state of reverie in which the mind wanders from idea to idea, nor is it a state of trance. It is true that other ideas will come to our attention during periods of meditation, but normally they will be relative to the *specific idea* contained in the meditation. So meditation would seem to be a most desirable way in which to practice the three steps— understanding, choice, and feeling and imagination—that are necessary for any law of life to express through us. Meditation should lead one to a state of mind in which action is paramount; it should be the urge that adds vitality to any objective action necessary to fulfill the desire or idea involved in the meditation itself.

The balance of this book is devoted to some definite suggestions and examples of *what meditation is* and *how one may use this* powerful idea to bring more of the potential of good into one's life. There is no magic in the words themselves. The apparent magic is in the feeling of acceptance of the ideas symbolized by the words.

You will find that each meditation deals with a specific affirmative idea. Each is designed to *induce a feeling* about that specific idea. They should not be considered formulas to be repeated by rote until they become meaningless. It would be good practice, however, to read them over with feeling and perhaps put the ideas into *your own words*. No one has a corner on words or Truth; your ideas should be as good as—if not better than—those stated.

To focus the attention on the central theme of each meditation, we have incorporated a quotation from the Bible. There is no *magic* in this; other sources would be just as effective. We just happen to believe that the Bible is one of the greatest books ever compiled on the morals and ethics necessary for a satisfactory way of life. Regardless of religious belief, you should be able to use the quotations as they are intended—to help center your attention on the idea involved.

In using these meditations, take time to enjoy them, feel their implication in connection with a given situation or desire in your life. In your imagination, sense how the ideas will work in your life; in your mind's eye, feel how it is to enjoy your new experiences.

Do not be afraid of becoming a little *emotional* in your meditation. Let a tear of happiness or gratitude flow now and then, if it is spontaneous. There is no danger in directed emotion. You are in control as long as your emotion is connected with your desire. What would actors, writers, inventors, or even mechanics really accomplish if they did not become emotionally enthused in their efforts?

Above all, realize that you are doing something to your mind that is providing the way through which the Basic Law of Life must give of Itself, abundantly, willingly, and lovingly. "Give it everything you have," and be at ease. Let go of strain, tension, or force and watch the *miracle of love* unfold in your life as you *move* with the law of love.

I BELIEVE IN GOD, THE LIVING SPIRIT ALMIGHTY

> *"Therefore being justified by faith, we have peace with God..."*
>
> *–Romans 5:1*

*M*y faith is justified.

❧ By nature, we instinctively believe in God. It may not be the idea of God believed in by our neighbor or blindly accepted as a child. Reason tells us there is some Power or Intelligence in and through all creation. The harmony and beauty of the Universe causes us to feel the presence of something warm and colorful behind, in, and through all life. This something has been called many names—Nature, God, Infinite Intelligence. As we sense within ourself the nearness of this Power, it becomes the Living Spirit Almighty within us. With our contemplation of the vast, wise, and intelligent activity of the Living Spirit as the Creative Power of life comes a feeling of the rightness of things. This larger vision draws us out of our *preoccupation* with the *less important* in our life. Uncertainties and fears are absolved in proportion to the larger vision. Realization of the presence of the Living Spirit Almighty establishes a new insight, a new sense of values, a new faith that sustains.

❧ My faith is justified as I realize the presence of Wisdom as the Living Spirit Almighty in all and through all.

I live by faith in the rightness of things, faith in the power that created and sustains me, faith in the Living Spirit as life within me and all people. Even though I do not know all the answers, what my neighbor thinks about me, what I shall be thinking or doing the next hour, week, or year, I release a sense of undue concern over these and other problems, uncertainties, and anxieties. My faith is justified as I see the basic good, integrity, and wisdom of God in and through all creation. *I rest secure* in that faith now.

GOD IS THE ONE ABSOLUTE AND ONLY POWER

*"Let every soul be subject unto the higher powers,
for there is no power but of God...."*

–Romans 13:1

 am one with all of the Presence and Power that there is.

ﻉ Everywhere we look, we see objective expressions, or things. We live in a universe of such objective expressions, *each related* in some way to the other. The magnitude and magnificence of that which we see, touch, taste, and experience defies our intellect to encompass. True, our reason leads us from effect back to cause, up to a point. The plant is caused by the seed. For example, this means that any effect is relative to and exists because there first was a cause for its being. Unhappy as well as happy experiences are caused by attitudes of mind. Somewhere in our analysis back from effect to cause, however, our reason tells us that ultimate *basic causation* or reason for being, we *cannot describe*. It must be accepted. Where and what is the intelligence behind the seed that grows the plant? What is the impulse, the activity of mind behind the happy or unhappy thinking? What is the intelligent, animating life principle that sustains our body and its activity? As the answers are not forthcoming and the intellect cannot carry us further, we can only conclude that there must be a Supreme Power and Wisdom that is simply Its own reason for being. In essence, It is indestructible Reality.

ﻉ I realize that behind all creation there is One Supreme Cause—I am aware of my oneness with the whole of life. The indestructibleness of the God-self or the Real me is assured. Effects, conditions, good times, so-called bad times, abundance and apparent limitations, states of health are all experiences in the relative objective world of effects. They are never things of themselves. That which caused them can change them. I turn in thought from any undesirable condition, knowing that it cannot sustain itself. Within me is the real God-intended person, the essence of Pure Spirit that never changes. Increasingly I feel the partnership, the sustaining Power with God, the one and only Presence. Increasingly assurance, peace of mind, and a sense of well-being objectifies in everything I do, say and experience. I am one with all the Presence and Power there is, for I am one with God.

GOD IS IN AND THROUGH ALL CREATION

"All things were made by Him; and without Him is not anything made that was made."

–John 1:3

Wherever I look I see God, the One and only Reality.

🙠 I sense God, the Living Spirit Almighty, in all things. The rippling brook is the murmuring chuckle of God. The lofty mountain peaks are the silent sentinels of God proclaiming God's placid power and might. The rhythm of the heavenly bodies and the mighty swell of the vast ocean express the harmony and exactness of God's Presence. The atomic activity, the harmony of the electrons revolving around their nucleus is akin to the beauty of the symphony of the celestial music of the spheres. In the rush of the traffic or the bargaining in the marketplace, I am aware of God expressing Itself. In all things I see God expressing Itself, yet I am aware that the Creator is always greater than the creation. The manifest universe is but the evidence of an infinite possibility for increased good, awaiting expression.

🙠 As I realize that God is the Creator and is constantly expressing through what is created, I am filled with a feeling of oneness with all of life. I realize that life is my life. I cannot be separated from it. It is all that I am. All sense of loneliness dissolves. Fear of people, conditions, past, present, and future, cannot withstand the understanding of my kinship with all because of the Fatherhood of God. Any condemnation of self or others with its accompanying feelings of guilt is dissipated forever. As I meet people in my daily living, there flows from me a warmth that returns as friendship, helpfulness, and a sense of well-being. Apparent confusion, either within me or in my contact with others, is replaced with *serenity* as I remind myself of the Presence of God in and through all things. I am grateful for the sense of well-being that comes to me as I remind myself constantly that God is all there is, and as I see God in and through all of life, I am awakened to the joy of living.

INFINITE SUBSTANCE IS THE BODY OF GOD

"Through faith we understand that the worlds were framed by the word of God, so that things which are seen were not made of things which do appear."
—*Hebrews 11:3*

$\mathcal{M}$y Body is a Divine Idea in Form.

જ There is no place in modern thinking for a *belief in basic duality.* Science has demonstrated that the material world is not something separate and apart from the world of unseen causes. This means that there is a *common source* from which all things come. The difference is in shape and form, but not in essence. All objective things are expressions of God. They are ideas made manifest and may rightly be called God in Form. We cannot say some things are spiritual and others are material. We do not live in a house divided against itself or a world of duality.

જ My body is a spiritual idea. The substance of my body is God substance. I bless my body as a thing of beauty. The Spirit of God is the creator and sustainer of every function of my physical being. Each organ of my body is a Divine idea. The life Principle, which maintains the harmony, balance, and vitality of my body is the activity of Spirit within me. That which would seem to be maladjustment or sickness is but a frustrated or limited expression of the life Principle within me. I know nothing can happen to God ideas in Reality. My body is a God idea, and behind any seeming restriction of expression there is wholeness and perfection. As I cease to condemn my body, as I refrain from a belief in duality, *I release the flood gates of life* to flow uninhibited through my physical being. I praise myself, my body, and all creation as I realize the One Presence in and through all. Tranquility and a sense of well-being envelops me now. Infinite Spirit expresses through me now and always as a Divine idea in form.

THE OMNISCIENCE OF GOD
IS THE SELF-KNOWINGNESS OF SPIRIT

"Known unto God are all his works from the beginning of the world."

$\mathcal{T}$he activity of Spirit is the Creative Principle of life.

&. "To God all things are possible." God Spirit or Infinite Wisdom is the Absolute Potential of all ideas. On the Universal scale, God creates through self-knowingness. Being absolute, there could be no resistance or opposition to the ideas of God. God speaks and it is done. The *basic principles* of nature are in themselves *ideas* of God in action. Mathematics, gravity, chemistry—yes, harmony and beauty—are ideas of Spirit creating, sustaining, and governing creation. They exist today, this minute, at every point of time and space because God Spirit is *omnipresent*. The self-knowingness within us is the self-knowingness of God expressing through us. Our spirit is the Spirit of God.

&. Quietly and with a sense of assurance, I am aware of the creative activity of Spirit in and through my life. I recognize negative experiences, apparent past mistakes only as resulting from a limited vision of my true relationship with the Infinite Presence. As I cease to give importance to the less desirable and let my thoughts and reactions to life become more Godlike, the obstructions to my greater good are dissolved. The Spirit within me, as me, is all-powerful. The God-self knows no opposition. As I free my mind from anxious thought of tomorrow, the creative self-knowingness of God makes straight the way. I am guided into paths of right action. I say and do the right thing at the right time. Discouragement and uncertainty flee from me as I realize my word is the presence and the activity of Spirit. I am sustained as I realize "With God all things are possible" and accept my Oneness with God.

GOD SPEAKS THROUGH EVERY PERSON

"And I have put my words in thy mouth...."
—*Isaiah 51:16*

We cannot escape our Divine heritage.

🔊 We ask ourselves, "What is it within me that thinks—recognizes—feels? Is it the body, the brain, or the nerves? These and similar questions will ultimately lead us in our thinking to where we have to say, honestly—"I really don't know, but this I do know—I can think, choose, feel, and consciously react to life. This is a self-conscious activity of mind within me."

Whatever it is that enables us to have this self-awareness must be the same in all people, for we perceive that all persons have the same ability. This is the basis for a feeling of oneness with all others. As to what it is that causes this to be, we can only answer, "being present in all people and being intelligent, it must be an expression of the Self-Knowingness of God or Spirit."

🔊 Recognizing the presence of God Spirit in all people, I feel a warm kinship with all people. Any sense of misunderstanding, hatred, confusion, or contention in my environment melts under the rays of *true love*, which is *genuine understanding*. I can understand another's motives as I understand myself. I can also understand myself more fully as I seek to understand others. As I realize humankind's spiritual origin, I forgive others and myself for any real or imagined wrong. Misunderstanding cannot prevail under this higher wisdom for I am aware that really that which I see in those whom I criticize is but some other aspect of myself. The seeds of hurt are within me, not another. As I turn in mind from the seeming hurt in my relationship with others and see the Real person in everyone, I can respect the opinions of others, even though they may differ from mine. There is no basis for quarrel or hurt as I realize all people partake of their Divine heritage according to their acceptance, for One Spirit speaks through each of us according to our understanding. I let Spirit speak through me and enrich my life in every way.

MY FUTURE IS SECURE

"Beloved, now are we the sons of God..."

—I John 1:2

At this moment, I am an immortal being.

❧ Deep in the heart of each one is the assurance that we are greater than anything that has ever happened to us. As the *eternal present moment* moves forward as experience, there is something within that whispers if we listen, "You are greater than any experience, for behind any experience is that which is experiencing." The artist is greater than the picture painted. This calming assurance in times of dire need establishes a faith based upon an instinctive feeling that our soul is but an expression of the Universal Soul of God. Our soul is immortal. Individualized experience seems to have finality, but that which experiences is greater than the sum total of all happenings. Our soul, that within us which feels and experiences, expands and progresses eternally. We did not create our soul. We are the way through which the Universal Artist, the Oversoul of God, expresses.

❧ At this moment I accept the past only as something that happened at that moment in time. I accept the future as that which is to be experienced. That which I inwardly feel about the past and the future governs my experience in this present moment. Right now my *conscious* and *unconscious* acceptance regarding the past, present, and future establishes what my future shall be. In and out through all experience, past, future, and present, is the *experiencer*. This is the Presence and Power that is greater than I am and yet is that which I am. It is that something within me which I did not create. It is the eternal soul of God within me, as me, forever expanding. At this moment I permit that which is greater than any past experience to uphold and sustain me. I contemplate the future in the certainty that I am an immortal and ever-expanding soul. My faith in the goodness of God and the eternal rightness of things is my assurance at this moment that my future must be, and is, secure. In this knowledge, I enter into the *livingness of this moment.*

THE KINGDOM OF HEAVEN IS WITHIN ME

"...behold the Kingdom of God is within you."
−Luke 17:21

I am one with, and have access to, all I shall ever need.

❧ A very wise person described God as the Presence and Power "whose circumference is nowhere and whose center is everywhere." The Infinite from which all things originate being all in all, there would be nothing outside or apart from It to separate or divide. In essence and in truth, that places the entire potential of God at any point in the time-space world.

As we grasp the significance of this truth, we can truly say the Kingdom of God is at the center of one's being. So-called objective things come into being through a *law of growth* or a step-by-step unfolding process. Things are ideas in form. Logically it would follow that within any idea is involved the process or law of growth by which it is to come into being. Within the Spirit, or Wisdom of God exists the Infinite potential of all ideas, both manifest or as yet unborn. The entire potential of God, being at any given point, means that right now the possibility of any desire and the law of growth by which it is to come into being is within us at this moment.

❧ My good develops according to the Divine law of growth. It is potentially completed in the Mind of God. I seek now first the Kingdom within and all things are added. My good becomes established according to God's Law of harmony and beauty. As God is everywhere present, even now as I speak my word for, and mentally embody, any specific good, the law of growth is at work wherever it should be to bring it into my experience. All ways and means are provided. My individual good is also *shared*, and all who contribute to its expression are *blessed*. I am one with God. The kingdom is within me. In confidence and faith, I know that all I shall ever need to express life fully is assured now in this moment. Calmly and with assurance I let Spirit guide and direct me into paths of fulfillment.

I INCREASINGLY BECOME AWARE OF
THE KINGDOM OF GOD

*"...the kingdoms of this world are become the
kingdoms of our Lord; and of his Christ; and he
shall reign forever and ever."*

–Revelation 11:15

*T*here is a beautiful loneliness within me that will not be
satisfied.

᠊᠊ Within everyone there is a deep yearning for something, someone, some experience. It apparently has nothing to do with any of the
objective experiences, for the moment a desire is fulfilled, once again
a growing void asserts itself. It is a Divine restlessness. As we become
aware of the Presence of God at the center of our being, the feeling
of loneliness that comes to all at times will not cause sadness or
apprehension. We will recognize it as a moment when all language
fails to explain and Infinite Spirit seeks to speak through us in the
language of God, which is love. As we become more conscious of the
Kingdom of God-good at the center of our being, so is the way
provided for more of the Divine potential to express in our lives.

᠊᠊ This moment I become more conscious of the love, harmony,
substance, and beauty of God. The Kingdom of the All lies within me.
I do not belittle past or present good, but see in it the foreshadowing
of greater possibility from the infinite storehouse. I do not fight or
resent those moments of apparent loneliness that seem to intrude,
even in the midst of friends and joyous experiences. I realize they
come to all, for all are children of the Most High. From these periods
of *divine restlessness* comes the calm assurance that I may become more
conscious of that which the Presence of God within me has lovingly
provided. That of which I become aware, I experience. I am not alone.
I cannot be lonely. With a new sense of freedom and wonder, I reach
out to receive the greater good. I now am more conscious of and
accept the never-ending greater possibility which is within me as it is
within all people, the Kingdom of God-good. Even in the midst of the
passing events and experiences, I am aware of the inner kingdom of
perfection at the center of my being. I know that the calm assurance
of harmony and *love* enters into my every act, and all whom I contact
feel it and are blessed.

DISCORD HAS NO PLACE IN UNIVERSAL GOD-MIND

*"Thou shalt hide them in the secret of thy presence
from the pride of man; thou shalt keep them secretly
in a pavilion from the strife of tongues."*
                                        –Psalms 31:20

*O*ur ultimate goal is freedom from discordant experiences.

❧ God must have created us with *freedom of choice*, if we are individuals. God of necessity must have created us perfect, but through power of choice we have used our individuality to seemingly deny our perfection. Some of our choices have been unwise in relation to our highest good and the good of others. In this sense we have unwisely used our God-nature, which cannot possibly know discord, to create unhappy and often hurtful experiences. Experience, *rightly understood*, is a good teacher. Everyone is traveling the road of unfoldment, or awakening to greater possibilities for self-giving and the rich rewards that automatically follow. No apparent discordant experience is meaningless as we make of it a *stepping-stone* to a greater awareness of the basic harmony of Reality.

❧ This day, this moment, I know no apparent discord can continue to cause me to feel unhappy or depressed. I am aware of my divine nature, my divine heritage. I thank God and am grateful that as an individual, freedom of choice is mine. Accepting that all experiences, past and present, are but guideposts, I learn more and more to depend on the Presence within me, which knows no discord, to use my freedom wisely. I make no quick or unwise decisions based solely on my intellect, opinion, or past experiences. With my intellect, I accept my partnership with the all-knowing God within me. With an unhurried sense of ease, I know right decisions will be made at the right time and that they will be right for myself and all concerned. I recognize the loving gift of God, my true freedom of choice. I seek to *consciously use* this power now and always to understand that discord is never the real, but a distorted shadow pointing the way to greater possibility. Knowing all experiences to be stepping-stones upward on the pathway of life, I move forward now, freed from any apparent discord, into a fuller acceptance of my good.

GOD'S PLAN FOR US IS PERFECT

"God is my strength and power; and he maketh my way perfect."

–II Samuel 22:33

n the eyes of the Infinite, all are alive and perfect.

❧ How many times have we cried out against fate and even God for allowing sickness to take hold of us? If God would only take *heed*, be *sympathetic* to our aches and pains, all would be well. In moments of clear insight, however, we realize that the nature of God, harmony, balance, beauty, would not permit God knowing illness. No, our sickness is not a part of God's plan for us. Our destiny under God is freedom from ills and discord. All will attain this freedom, for *God has no favorites*. We think of the experience of illness as being real until we feel better. It then becomes but a memory. The wisdom of life has set us free, because we have permitted it to do so. Many states of health have been proclaimed as incurable until someone discovered the cure. Wisdom again has released us from fear and the condition that caused it. The whole process is not bringing God into a state of sympathetic understanding, but rather in our understanding of love and embodying more of the Divine Infinite nature, *we permit* it to be revealed and expressed through us. This is the Divine plan for us, that we shall express and unfold in awareness of Truth. As we each are made of the stuff of God, in God's image and likeness, our freedom and increasing Good is assured.

❧ Because *I am, God is* and because God is, I am. I now emphatically state and know that sickness is not real, only an experience. I rejoice that God knows not sickness. I am thankful that wisdom, as love, is the healing power of any discordant condition. I do not fight disease or seek God's help in *combating* any state of ill health. I do realize that freedom from any discord is automatically God's help as I permit God's Wisdom to become understanding of the Truth about my state of ill health. I do realize the Truth—that freedom from discord is God's plan for me, for the nature of the Infinite cannot know discord. I am not anxious or impatient. With *serenity* I know that Spirit responds to my need in any way and through any channel for the greater wisdom that will free me into perfect health. It is being done. All is working to that end. Under God's plan for me and for all people, it is already done. I am radiant with health, happiness, wonder, and interest as I, at this moment, let Perfection, which is God, express through me. Health is mine now.

ALL LIFE IS GOD IN ACTION

*"And hath made of one blood all nations of men for
to dwell on all the face of the earth..."*

–Acts 17:25

*T*here is an unseen thread of life that unites all humankind.

ᐓ No one has seen the essence of life at any time. Nor have we seen God. This need not startle us or cause us concern. No one can comprehend the Infinite or picture the Absolute Reality behind all things. We do know there is God, because we see and experience what God does. Life is the animating principle within each of us. It is the intelligent activity of Spirit, because it knows how to perpetuate itself and express in us as body. Every function of our physical body or activity in the body of our affairs, is the presence and power of life in action. Each of us in expressing the one life—God-life. There could not be our *individual life* and a different individual life for everyone else. This would be as illogical as to suppose there could be an individual air for each of us to breathe. Each is united by the common bond of the one life. All humankind is united. In a sense, some part of each is some part of the other. As we realize the truth of his interrelationship with others, and to the degree that we do, the causes of hatred, dissension, frustration, loneliness, and the things that keep us from experiencing our greater good, are lessened.

ᐓ At this moment, I sense the warmth and glow of vital life within me. I trust and reverence this life, because I realize it must be God-life expressing as me. This warmth and vital enthusiasm of life action I sense in all other persons. A warm kinship is experienced within me as I realize that we are united, bound together in the One Life. It is impossible for me to feel lonely or alone. The seeming differences of opinion, beliefs and modes of expression in others are understood as I realize that behind each is the One Life. This warmth that I feel toward all humankind is felt by all who come my way. I would not hurt another, for I would not *knowingly hurt myself*. I would not bear false witness, condemn, nor appropriate another's good, for I realize I would be doing these things to some part of myself. I feel at home in my world and a sense of warmth and ease with all whom I contact, for I realize the thread of God-life unites and sustains each one.

GOD IS WHERE I AM AT ALL TIMES

"Whither shall I go from thy spirit...?"
–Psalms 139:7-10

*O*ur search for God is ended as we realize the unity of all things.

🍃 Sometimes, in the midst of a problem arising through our association with others, in seeking an answer to our need, we seem to get further away from a solution. We don't know which way to turn. Guidance apparently eludes us. At such times we are liable to *beseech* and *plead* with a power away off somewhere, we know not where. We feel God must be reached through a high state of consciousness, because God must be above the mundane things of life. God surely has no time for our relatively small problems. So we mentally reach out in our seeking for the warmth of response from the Infinite, which everything within us tells us we need. As we come to realize the underlying unity of all things, we awaken to the fact that God is within ourself. As this truth becomes real, the *search and beseechment are over* and done. Regardless of what is happening on the outside, the All-powerful, All-knowing Wisdom is within. The assurance that God does *know* about us and *cares* comes with this feeling of closeness, as we bask in the warmth of this newly found intimacy.

🍃 Today I realize that because God is everywhere, God is within me right now. No longer is the feeling of doubt or separation in my mind. No longer do I need to search, petition, and beseech in order to *commune* with the One Presence. In my quiet moments, yes, at *this* very moment, I am sustained. The realization of my true value and worth in the Divine scheme of things releases the anxiety and doubt of things that are and things to come. It is true we are never left without a witness. I *bless* my every thought as the activity of Spirit within me. I am *thankful* for every experience, for I sense the Presence within me as the great experiencer. Poise and peace, which cannot be shaken, sustains and goes before me for I know my search for God is ended. The high potential of God lies within me and in all people. I await with joyous anticipation the *unfoldment* of God-ideas as experience ever expressing in my life.

THE PERSONALNESS AND WARMTH OF GOD
SUSTAINS ME ALWAYS

"God is our refuge and strength, a very present help in trouble."

–Psalms 46:1

*T*he Infinite Presence responds to me; I cannot be alone.

• Our intellect tells us that there must be an underlying Law governing and supporting life in all its activities. We may call this the Law of God and assume It must be *exact* and *harmonious* in Its *response* of action, else there would be chaos. The Law of the Lord is perfect. The intellect, as important as it is, never by itself completely satisfies us. It is too often cold and impersonal. The intellect directs us, however, to maintain certain reactions or feelings within ourself that are so important in one's living. Our intellect tells us of God as Principle, or Law, which functions with exactness of absolute "justice without judgment." We are not satisfied, however, with this explanation alone. It is cold. We long for warmth and response on the part of God. We want to feel that in some manner God *understands* our needs and responds *lovingly*. Our intellect does not permit us to think of God in the form of a person, for that would be limiting. We can understand, however, that God is the *source* of all these things. We can know with certainty that the attribute of personalness must be an aspect of God because of the exactness, care, and loving provision for all God's creation. The very personalness that we experience as we converse or communicate with others may well be the personalness of God made manifest. As we dwell with feeling on this intellectual understanding, we sense, as we commune with God in a personal way, that God's Presence, Power, and Wisdom must respond to us. As we are convinced of the personalness of God responding to us as law, according to our needs, can we not feel the answer well up within us, "Yes, I know the answer to your problem. I will sustain and guide you in all things."

• I know God becomes personal to me as I turn to It in complete *faith* and *love*. Even though I have made unwise decisions and mistakes, complete forgiveness is mine as I recognize the Presence of Love, as God, within, as me. Forgiveness is of *my own doing*, for God *does not condemn* us. As I now turn to God with an open mind, it is as though an unseen presence takes my hand and sustains me. I cannot be separated from my good (God) even though events may have caused me to feel separated. Warmth and a sense of loving response comes to me as I "let go and let God." Words of gratitude flood my being. "It is good to be alive." Never again shall I doubt, never again feel alone, for today I walk with God—now and always—as I feel God's indwelling Presence at all times.

GOD IS TRUTH

"He is the Rock, his work is perfect; for all his ways are judgment; a God of truth and without iniquity, just and right is he."

–Deuteronomy 32:4

Behind all creation is truth that never changes.

ॐ If we are to worship God, we must worship Him in Spirit and in Truth. To *worship* is to *commune*, to feel close to, to understand, and to sense an understanding response. Much of our groping for security, our frustrated desire for more of the good things of life, arises through mistaking observable facts for truth. Facts are objective appearances and, to our *physical senses*, the way things seem to be. If we accept the obvious and the objective as basic truth, we become fixed in our concept and limited to our resulting frustrated ideas. If we observe our own lack of money and judges according to the apparent facts, we will find many reasons for remaining *rooted* in lack. We may say, "To have money, I must do as others have done to get it." The truth is, no two persons are alike, so we cannot imitate another. Or we may say, "If I have abundant supply, someone else will be deprived of their good." Being innately good and desiring to harm no one, this in itself is a good mental treatment to germinate seeds of limitation. God is Infinite Supply, God is Truth. The *fact* may seem to say, "Money is the root of all evil," a frustrating contemplation, for no one wants to consciously embrace evil. The *truth* is, money is God substance and symbolizes, when properly understood, the logical outcome of self-giving. If thought of as a means of personal power or the means to control others or if used in any manner hurtful to ourselves or another, it could produce evil or unhappiness. Understanding that apparent facts are not things of themselves but results of how we have *viewed* the truth basic to the fact frees us from fixed experiences that are hurtful.

ॐ This day I am freed from the worship of facts and through

understanding embrace the truth that is God. More money passes through my hands as I realize I am the way through which God-substance circulates. I let go of the limiting concepts. The truth is that *money represents self-giving*. Knowing this, I accept that opportunity for self-giving according to my talents is always at hand. Through spending, I open the way for more money to pour itself through me. I bless that which I receive and I bless that which I give or spend. Happiness, richer living, flows from me and returns to me as I now release the frustration of apparent facts and embody the truth about money. I am the way through which Spirit as substance pours itself. I am blessed by this activity of Spirit. All whom I contact are blessed as I realize the truth that God is not a God of limitation but of abundance. In this Spirit of Truth, I speak my word, knowing that the God of Truth and Justice rewards me openly and good is mine to use and share. I accept my good now.

THE WISDOM OF GOD PROCLAIMS ITSELF THROUGH ME

> *"That ...the Father of Glory, may give unto you the spirit of wisdom and revelation in the knowledge of him."*
>
> *–Ephesians 1:17*

*W*e are spiritual beings.

* We have been told that "humans were created perfect, but they have sought out devious ways." To be spiritual is the most natural thing in the world. The very nature of humankind is Spirit, for by the *Spirit*, or *self-knowingness* of God, were we created. This means that the body is a spiritual idea. As such, we should praise it. The life force or instinctive life principle sustaining the body is the wisdom or voice of God proclaiming itself as a divine idea. We should trust and praise in action. We are one with God, sons and daughters of the Most High, spiritual beings. As such, we should *praise ourselves* and feel the warmth of *gratitude* toward God within ourselves and all people. Through envy, hatred, force, strain, shortsightedness, etc, we seek out devious ways opposed to our real God-self. By giving recognition to these negative attitudes, strength, vitality, and a sense of ease are kept from expressing through us. The resulting discomfort or disease is not something real. It is the experience resulting from a limited use of that which itself is perfect and complete.

❧ At this moment and at any moment during the day or night, I thank God that I can say, "It is good to be alive." I am a spiritual being. The wisdom of Spirit flows through me as instinctive life. Thank God I can have complete faith and confidence that God-life within me, as me, guides, directs, and regulates the many functions of my body. I praise this spiritual action within me as I *praise my body* as the temple of the Living Spirit of God. I am not disturbed or fearful of that which appears to be disease. It is not a thing of itself. Through praise and blessings of my true spiritual self, the limited or frustrated action is removed, permitting the *healing action* of the wisdom of Spirit to take over. I *rest in action* as I realize I am a Spiritual Being, recognizing and expressing the Wisdom of God.

TRUTH INSPIRES AND SUSTAINS MY MARRIAGE

"With all lowliness and meekness, with long suffering, forbear one another in love; endeavoring to keep the unit of the Spirit in the bond of Peace."
—*Ephesians 4:2, 3*

Everyone is in partnership with God.

❧ Any partnership founded on the basis of mutual support and harmonious effort is a successful enterprise. Each partner supplies some need to the particular expression involved. In our human relationships, the realization that everyone is in partnership with the indwelling Presence of God is ever helpful. Our individual partnership with God represents the way through which God expresses through creation. In this sense *God needs us.* The infinite potential of God supplies that which we intellectually lack but which we need for successful self-expression. A recognition of one's Divine Partnership is the source of inspiration necessary to guide us in our human relationships. In this sense *we need God.* This partnership of *mutual need* is particularly emphasized in the most satisfying of all human partnerships, marriage. If we recognize in our marriage partner that each is a dispenser of the Divine gifts, giving of oneself in love, each shall not only experience more good but be a more *complete* and *whole* individual. It will not be a matter of *possessiveness* or *domination*, but a partnership founded on truth and understanding, inspired by wisdom, love, and mutual helpfulness.

❧ I recognize in myself and all people the indwelling Presence of Truth. God is my partner, inspiring me in all that I do. In all of my relationships with others, I recognize the expression of Divine cooperation. I recognize my marriage as a partnership inspired by *truth* and *love*. Through recognition of my partnership with God, I am inspired to do, say and express in such a way that my marriage partner shall receive that which is necessary to make life more complete and meaningful. This I shall expect to receive in my life also. There is no jealousy or envy in my marriage relationship, for I recognize in it a partnership of two individuals dedicated to the expression of their Divine partnership with God, Good. Truth, wisdom, and love inspire thoughtfulness, consideration, and helpfulness and assure the success of my partnership of marriage.

UNIVERSAL SPIRIT IS THE SOURCE OF ALL IDEAS

"For the word of God is quick and powerful and sharper than any two-edged sword..."

–Hebrews 4:12

*M*y thoughts are ideas of God expressing.

❧ Ideas are *symbols* of truth taking form. They express through people as thought and action. The Spirit of God is the infinite source and potential of all ideas. As we sense our oneness with God, so do we realize that *we are the way* through which God-ideas express. Many times, opinions and beliefs interfere with the clear translation of God-ideas into God-like experiences. This does not mean that God Spirit lacks or is limited. A limited idea is our *limited interpretation* of an *unlimited* idea of Spirit. Inharmony is a limited concept of Infinite Harmony. Lack and limitation would be only an inhibited expression of the infinite potential of the abundance of God. Confusion and upsetness of mind is not truth but only failure to embody or understand the beauty and harmony that governs all creation. We cannot change, alter, or coerce the Infinite to suit our whims. We can expand our concept of the Infinite and provide the way for Spirit, the source of all ideas, to pour Itself in an increased way through us.

❧ Today I become more aware of my oneness with Infinite Spirit. I speak my word for an increased expression of harmony and happiness in my life and affairs. I know that which appears as unhappiness or confusion in my life symbolizes only my limited acceptance of the divine harmony of God nature. I know that Spirit, complete, whole, and harmonious, is within me and every person. All ideas necessary to bring into being any good (God) thing in my life are available to me. I move from moment to moment with a sense of *ease* and *peace of mind*, for I realize I am the way through which God's ideas are symbolized in objective form. As my thoughts and ideas become more inclusive by seeing God everywhere and in everything, I provide the way for Infinite Spirit to pour Itself richly through my every thought, word, and deed. Today my mind is receptive to a clearer vision of the storehouse of God-ideas that lies within me. As I let my thoughts symbolize the divine nature of God—good—I embrace in every way *the more abundant life*.

THE LAW OF THE LORD IS PERFECT

"The law of the Lord is perfect...."

–Psalms 19:7

The Law of God-mind is the activity of Spirit.

◆ Just as there is Universal Spirit, the potential of all ideas, so is there Universal Law by which God-ideas become manifest. This Law of God is the *potential* of all *power* and *action*. It is exact and infinitely wise in knowing what to do, but awaits the ideas of Spirit in order to act. Once given the idea, it cannot, by its nature, refuse to act. In this way the spiritual ideas of God cannot help but manifest, for in reality there can be *no resistance to God*. Thus, the Universe and all God expressions come into being and are sustained by the Divine Idea expressing Itself through the Law of Mind, which must respond. This is the creative process by which the Law of God, by its action, becomes the activity of Spirit, to produce Its ideas in form. Our words, thoughts, and ideas through this activity of God-mind in us objectify themselves in our experience if we accept them. The Law of the Lord, being the activity of Infinite Spirit, is perfect and complete in its action and accepts no resistance.

◆ I speak my word for my good, knowing that the Law of the Lord is perfect. Whatever my desire may be, friendship, love, appreciation,

I know it is a *spiritual desire*. In it there is no hurt or harm to another or to myself. As my desires are based on good (God) ideas, I know there can be no resistance to them. While I may not see or understand all that is to take place in order to bring my good into being, I am never discouraged or anxious. My desire as I request it through prayer and spiritual mind treatment is the activity of Spirit within me. The Law of God-mind assures its outcome. Once spoken, believed, and accepted by me, my word acts independently of my belief, past experience, apparent lack, or failure. I rest in the knowledge and am sustained by the realization that the Law of the Lord is perfect. As the activity of the all-knowing Spirit, it inspires, guides and directs me into paths of accomplishment. This moment I wait upon the Law (Lord) with a *calm expectancy* and complete assurance of my good.

I AM SURROUNDED BY AND ONE WITH CREATIVE MIND

> *"I will pray with the Spirit, and I will pray with understanding."*
> —Corinthians 14:15

*T*he language of God is affirmative.

   To know that the Law of God responds creatively to our thoughts and beliefs provides a basis for faith. This response is affirmative always. God simply affirms or agrees with us. We have complete faith that should we place our hand in water, it will become wet. There is an unhesitating, affirmative response on the part of water. It never denies us nor argues with us. So it is with the Creative Principle of Mind. There is no hesitancy in its response. It does not argue but unhesitatingly receives the impress of our thought and belief and acts upon it. It is not necessary to understand how the water makes us wet. *We accept that it does—we act as though it will—and it happens.* Our only part in the procedure is to supply the opportunity for water to make us wet. Creative Mind acts upon our thoughts, never arguing. We do not have to know the *how*, or the *why*, or even if it will. If we go into the water it will make us wet simply because it is its nature to do so. It is the nature of creative God-mind to respond to us, and we may rest assured that *it knows* the how and the why involved. Where do we contact Creative Mind? It is everywhere present, within everyone, within us, acting and responding at this moment as we read this statement. God's language is affirmative through Creative Mind. God's response to us is affirmative in its effect in our lives as we turn to God, believing and thinking in an affirmative manner. Our faith is strengthened as we know that God is constantly *affirming for us that which we affirm about ourselves.*

🐙 I know I am at this moment at one with the Creative Mind of God. God in Its infinite love cannot deny me anything that I wish to accept. His affirmative response is always active through me. The life that I live, that which I have and experience, are gifts that I receive through *my asking.* Undesirable, unpleasant, or unhappy experiences I recognize as gifts that I have *unthinkingly* or *unknowingly* accepted. My faith is not weakened by this realization, but my trust in the affirmative response of God is strengthened. Through the same Creative Mind I can now, in faith, turn from the undesirable acceptances and, through a new affirmative request, render them ineffective and inoperative. As I see God in all things, my requests, thoughts, and beliefs become affirmative. As my thoughts become centered on the wisdom, love, and beauty of God, so do affirmative gifts come into my experience. They come from any necessary source, for God is in all and through all. I reject affirmatively anything that would deny my good, knowing God affirms my affirmation. I *let* these good things *happen to me now.*

GOD MIND IS THE HEALING POWER WITHIN ME

"The tongue of the wise is health."
                                                –Proverbs 12:18

*H*ealth of body is our natural expression.

🐙 Creative Mind, the Law of God, does respond to our convictions, beliefs, and acceptances. The knowledge that life is the activity of Spirit, and Spirit is the source of Divine ideas, permits the healing power of *intelligent life action* to flow through us uninhibited. That our body is a divine idea is known in the mind of God. God created it and provides, through the activity of Spirit, everything necessary to sustain it. Through our acceptance of ideas of sickness, whether they be our own, those of someone else, or a generally accepted belief, we interfere with the "ease" of life action of body, and "disease" is the result. Knowing this, we cannot accept disease as a truth but a lie, *masquerading as truth.* The healing of disease through spiritual mind treatment does not mean that we *create* or bring the healing power to action. It is already there. Any healing process consists of removing the blocks of frustration and hindrances to life's action so that once again the spiritual idea that created us will sustain and express through us as perfect body. As we turn our attention from the appearance by knowing that even though it is a fact of experience, it is not real, and embrace the truth in spite of any belief, past or present, the healing presence of God takes over. It was there all the time—it is there now—awaiting permission to express through us.

In the light of my understanding that my *natural expression* of life is *perfect health*, I now claim my rightful heritage. This word removes the obstructions to the activity of pure Spirit in and through me as perfect life. Every thought or acceptance of the reality of disease is neutralized and cast out. Past experiences, beliefs of myself and others have, of and by themselves, no power to cause disease. I toss them out as I would a bad dream upon awakening to the truth of the waking moment. I am not concerned with the healing process. God-mind responds to my acceptance that perfect life is *natural* and *normal* for me. The healing of my body is automatic as I now accept that the Spirit within guides and directs my every thought and conviction. Everything necessary to clarify my mind, remove any obstruction and reveal my true state of being, I am *impelled* to realize and accept. I am uplifted, strengthened, and vitalized now and always as I realize that health is my natural state, and nothing can happen to it. God *in me, as me,* is perfect life that expresses as ease of body at this moment.

INFINITE SPIRIT CANNOT BE CONGESTED

"The Lord will perfect that which concerneth me."
−Psalms 138:8

Creative Mind's healing action circulates freely in me.

Healing action is normal action. Normal action is God action. If one becomes congested in thought and emotion, normal action of body is interfered with. Fear causes one to secrete *powerful stimulants* within the body to *fight the source of fear*. When fear is vague or unfounded, a continued state of heightened stimulation or circulation is the result. Likewise, certain mental states of anxiety, or an unhappy or depressed frame of mind may cause glandular secretions that would slow the circulation and lower the vitality, and congestion is the result. All of this causes discomfort and so-called disease. As one realizes that Infinite Spirit, being always in a state of harmony and balance, cannot be congested or overactive, one takes a different attitude toward one's trouble. A realization of our oneness with God, knowing that Creative Mind within us seeks always to express through us according to its nature of *harmony, balance,* and *right action,* automatically releases the pressure of excessive trying or tension on our part. To know that God, or life, *is for us* is a tranquilizer for the overwrought and a needed natural stimulant for the depressed. We must practice the presence of *peace* in our thinking. To do so is to cleanse our minds and bodies of stagnant impurities. Thinking on love and a sense of inner security and seeking to dwell on a peaceful, balanced action of life within the body is good curative and *preventive* medicine. Say many times a day, "The protection of the Infinite All-wise Spirit upholds and sustains me now and always."

೩ This word that I speak is the law of my life. Divine circulation of spiritual ideas governs every thought and action. Peace flows from the center of my being. Regardless of appearances, as harmony moves in, fear, uncertainty, and any overaction or inaction move out of my experience. Right where the congestion or overaction seems to be, this word is effective. My blood circulates normally, stimulating normally and eliminating normally. I am content to accept my good, the divine and guiding action of Spirit, without question. I do not have to establish balance in my body or affairs; it already is, for I am, by nature, a Divine Being. I do not *fight* or *contend.* As I keep my thoughts affirmative and expectant of good, I *let* Creative Mind's healing action flow through me now.

THE RHYTHM OF LIFE IS THE EXPRESSION
OF DIVINE IDEAS

"Behold, I make all things new."
—*Revelations 21:5*

Every organ of my body is a divine idea of God.

೩ God created the world and looked upon it and saw that it was good. In the first chapter of Genesis we find this is the key thought in the Bible story of creation. God is the only Creator and God is good. The body of a human is a wonderful and complete idea. Every organ within it is a perfect idea. *We did not create a single cell within our body.* An Infinite Wisdom within us created and sustains every action. Each organ has a *purpose* that Spirit knows all about. We need not question the purpose or doubt the perfection of our body. It is true that through anxiety, doubt, and fear, we can hinder the full, harmonious expression of God-life and seemingly impair the functioning of certain organs. We can believe what others tell us of sickness and can dwell on our own past physical ailments. According to our *belief* is it done unto us. A more complete belief will take precedence over a lesser belief. As we recognize the body and each organ as a God idea, created and sustained by Infinite Wisdom, anxiety lessens, *healing adjustment* takes place. There is healing in *blessing* the body, its every organ and action. The intelligent response to an attitude of blessing is often seemingly miraculous.

ᐳ   This day I bless my body and its every organ. I say to myself, "It's good to be alive, it's good to feel good." I feel good as I release the anxiety about myself and any particular organ. Creative Mind—God Intelligence—knows how to sustain every organ in harmonious wholeness. I do not doubt the action of Spirit within me to maintain harmony, vitality, and strength. I do not struggle or sympathize with what others say about being ill, nor feel I have to contend with any past experiences of illness in my own life. I turn away from seeming imperfection by knowing *God ideas cannot be destroyed*, weakened, or impaired. I accept in complete faith that as I sense every organ as a Divine concept, God will do all that is necessary to reestablish wholeness and vitality of action wherever it is needed.

MY WORKING CONDITIONS EXPRESS
MY INNER ACCEPTANCE OF LIFE

> *"See that ye love one another with a pure heart fervently."*
>
> *–I Peter 1:22*

*T*hrough the nature and power of God-mind to respond in love to our desires, we control our affairs.

ᐳ   With our acceptance of the fact that we are one with God-mind, which is constantly doing for us and giving to us "as we believe," comes the realization that never again can we say, "It was fate that it happened." Or, "Some people are lucky, but not I." Not can one say, "If I had so-and-so's opportunities, I, too, could be surrounded by wealth and friends." Much as we would like to blame our state of conditions upon some outside source, once we have affirmed our oneness with the action of the Creative Mind of God to do our bidding, we must assume that we are in a great measure responsible for our world of experience. In this way, through our inner thought, we are enabled to affect that which goes on around us. Controlling conditions in this manner does not mean *controlling other people*. This would be using the Law unwisely. It is not necessary and doubtful if actually it can be done. If we are experiencing unhappiness and confusion, we do not have to change the nature of people or the way they act. Our problem lies within our own thought. If Creative Mind responds to our belief and acceptance, and if we desire to change conditions in our experience, we must first *mentally accept and inwardly unify* with harmonious working and environmental conditions. See the harmony. Accept it. Live it. "The signs will follow." The power and wisdom of Creative Mind will do the work. In the process of bringing harmony out of confusion, happiness out of hurt, people may change—our job may change—we may change—but first, our *inner acceptances* or beliefs *must change*. Understanding love, free from domination and desiring only the best for all concerned, is a good pattern to abide by in changing any beliefs.

᠘᠘ This day I realize that I am one with Creative Mind, God-mind. I see in those conditions that are unhappy or confusing in my work, outer reflections of an inner state of awareness. Regardless of who or what I may feel to be the cause, I know this word I now speak has the *power to change* whatever is necessary for the establishment of harmony and right action. Therefore I clear my thought of any hurt or desire to hurt anyone. I am freed from any feeling of jealousy or envy. I know I am always in my right place, taking nothing that belongs to another. As I desire only good for all with whom I am associated, under the Law of God-mind *only good returns to me*. I do not contend nor outline but let the all-knowingness of God Spirit possess me and direct me in all ways. I do not change others but know Infinite Spirit now brings about any change needed to establish harmony in my working conditions and in my affairs. I am constantly aware of understanding love, which instantly moves in to neutralize any attempt of past hurtful ideas to assert themselves. I let this power of love control me and in turn flood my whole environment, and in this *action of love there can be no hurt*.

CREATIVE MIND ESTABLISHES
UNDERSTANDING IN MY LIFE

*"Understanding is a wellspring of life unto him
that hath it."*

–Proverbs 16:22

 understand and am understood by all whom I contact.

   To understand another does not mean that we have to agree with all that they say or do. Understanding, however, is the basis for getting along with people in our daily contacts. Friction, bickering, and confusion in our environment cannot exist where there is understanding. As we understand our own nature, as we realize that *we are the way* through which Creative Mind, or Spirit, expresses, and as we recognize our God-given *freedom of choice*, our understanding of others increases. In reality we see in others what we know to be true about ourself. We have been told, "Know thyself." Also, if we are true to ourselves, we cannot be false to anyone. Proclaiming our own divinity and seeing that same divinity in all whom we contact is the basis for harmony and agreement in our human relationships. Differences of opinion, action, and beliefs lose their hurtful effect and power to confuse or make us unhappy as we *respect* the divinity within *ourselves* and *all persons.*

   I understand and am understood by all whom I contact. I do not ignore apparent weaknesses in myself or others. I do not quarrel with myself or others over apparent mistakes. Through my understanding of my true and divine nature, this day I let Creative Mind establish understanding in my life. I respect my own divinity and know Infinite Spirit governs my thought about and reaction to all whom I meet. Condemnation or malicious thoughts have no place in my thinking. I understand them for what they are and instantly turn from them. *Understanding*, which is *true love*, melts and dissipates anything unlike itself. Even in apparent disagreements, there can be no hurt. Divine adjustment takes place constantly in all that I do and in my relationships with others. I rest secure in each and every moment in the knowledge that the light of Spirit precedes me in all things. The understanding and love that I feel at this moment *returns to me* from all whom I contact, establishing harmony in my life. Only good goes from and only good returns to me. I am persistent in my affirmation and joyous in my expectancy.

SUPPLY SYMBOLIZES GOD SUBSTANCE IN FORM

"For whosoever hath, to him shall be given, and he shall have more abundance."

–Matthew 13:12

*T*here is no debt, only balance, in my supply.

All objective form is the result of Spirit giving *shape to God substance* through the Law of Creativity. Spirit contains the potential of all ideas. The infinite possibility of good is limited only by the form involved as the idea to be expressed. This is the answer as to why God will permit poverty in some families and an abundance in others. It is not because God is limited or could possibly desire limitation for anyone. The Infinite being limitless, debt and lack could not be God-intended. Limitation, whether experienced in persons, families, or nations, could only be the result of small ideas being provided for the limitless to flow through. The light globe is a limited expression of the *potential possibility* of electricity. Thought patterns of poverty, lack, and limitation must give way to the expanded awareness as we realize our access to and the availability of a greater good. In this new awareness it seems as though the Infinite Presence whispers. "All that I have is thine." So long as we believe in the burdens and necessity of debt, we will fail to experience the greater abundance that has been so *lovingly provided.*

At this moment, I turn within and am filled with a sense of security through a realization of my oneness with all good, harmony, truth, and balance. I know this divine balance is governing my supply. Spirit guides and directs me into paths of *right action* and *correct decisions.* Any past or present belief in the imbalance of debt is now eliminated from my thought. I know it is the Father's good pleasure to give me of His infinite supply. I open my mind to the influx of those ideas which become symbolized as God-substance in the form of money. The balance of giving of myself and receiving back from life all that I need is maintained at all times. I welcome the opportunity to express and know that the balance, as appreciation and compensation, is *automatic* under the Law of Divine Balance. I am never called upon to feel I must spend more than I have. The burden of debt and its power to limit has no place in my thinking. Freed from anxiety, I move from moment to moment with increasing faith my good is ever available to me, for I am one with the source of all good—God.

I give to receive and receive to give. As my consciousness (mental awareness) grows, both the receiving and giving are increased to meet my needs. I bless the giving as I release my gift, and I bless the gifts returned to me from life and others. In *gratitude*, I know that under God's Law of Balance, all my needs to insure a more joyous, happy, and abundant life are assured.

THE HARMONIOUS ACTIVITY OF SPIRIT
GOVERNS ANY CHANGE IN MY LIFE

> *"The Lord is my rock and my fortress and my deliverer; my God, my strength in whom I will trust."*
>
> *–Psalms 18:2*

*T*he stability of God is my rock of faith.

ɞ Our *reaction* to any change in our life is colored by and largely governed by our thought and feeling about life itself. If our sense of security is unduly placed in *objective things*, we shall *resist* change in any form. If one thinks security rests in the salary earned in one's present position, they will unknowingly, perhaps, resist any change indicated in their work. If one is convinced that good depends on a certain person or group of persons or must come through certain designated channels, resistance to change will usually follow. Any set resistance to change signifies an *inner resistance* to life. The very nature of Spirit, as life, is to express itself in many ways and through many channels. It is the nature of God to express Itself through the unfoldment of Its ideas. *Nothing in nature is static.* Being divine beings, partaking of the Divine nature, no part of us remains static. Our bodies, our thoughts, and our feelings are constantly changing. Our awareness of life and our relationship to it certainly changes with passing events. To resist change stifles growth. As we appreciate our divinity, feel our oneness with Spirit, and sense the harmonious activity of life within ourselves, our resistance becomes less, and we will let change take place easily. This will logically and easily follow the inner feeling of a *day-by-day* unfoldment of an expanding awareness, leading us to a happier and fuller expression of life.

ɞ Any thought of fear of change is at this moment removed from my thinking. I am aware now and always that the presence of Spirit guides and directs my every thought, act, and feeling in paths of unfoldment and self-expression. I recognize the divine nature of change in my life. I do not *outline* or say exactly what that change shall be. As I dismiss negative comparisons with what others do or what I have done, I move easily and harmoniously into new experiences. I do not accept the necessity of abrupt or hurtful changes. As I feel the presence of the divine nature at the center of my being, I am filled with *courage* and *strength*. Any resistance to life situations and conditions disappears as I now realize the activity and harmony of Spirit increasingly expressing Itself through me. I am not hurried nor do I feel impatient in making decisions; they will be guided only by a desire for good and right action for myself and all concerned, "knowing all things work together for good."

GOD ETERNALLY EXPRESSES LIFE AND LOVE THROUGH ALL PERSONS

"For as the Father hath life in Himself, so hath he given in the Son to have life in himself."

–John 5:26

I am increasingly aware of the goodness and loving-kindness of God in all people.

As we observe our day-to-day actions and our mental reactions to life, it is natural to conclude that we are individuals with *power* to *choose*. We also realize that our choices, in some manner, affect our environment as well as our conditions of health and our material supply. Realizing that this power of dominion in our lives is possible only because of a higher Presence and Power that responds to our choices and acceptances, we make it possible for *greater good* to move into our life through the same power of choice. As we come to understand that all persons have their roots in, and partake of, this all-inclusive good, we begin to feel the support of the *loving-kindness* and the sustaining Presence of Life, God-life, eternally expressing Itself in all and through all. This larger vision reveals unified kinship with all persons. Truly we are not isolated individuals, but individualized expressions of the One Life, which is God-good. Loneliness and feelings of separation fade as we realize that every person is one with, and motivated by, the One Presence that constantly responds to us in love.

A sense of *false* responsibility for making things happen through force or will power is eliminated, for we choose to let the power of God-mind do for us. The door to happiness, joy, and a richer life experience is opened as we recognize the eternal living Presence of loving-kindness, the goodness of God-life flowing through us and through all humanity.

◆ At this moment I am aware of the presence of God expressing through me as loving-kindness and eternal goodness. I am aware that the gift of every good thing has been made through the Divine givingness of the nature of God. Spirit moves through me now to remove any obstructions that my short-sightedness may have created. I feel love and understanding going out from me and returning to me. No longer do I fret or become anxious if I do not *intellectually comprehend* all things. I am relieved of the frustrating responsibility of outlining how and through what channel my good shall come to me. I move and live from *moment to moment*, knowing that I am sustained by the eternal givingness of life moving through me, guiding and directing me in all of my contacts with life. All things are working together for good, because I am one with the eternal goodness of God.

BECAUSE I BELIEVE IN GOD, I BELIEVE IN MYSELF

> *"Cast thy burden upon the Lord and he shall maintain thee."*
>
> *–Psalms 55:22*

I am one with the Infinite Spirit of God and the Soul of the Universe.

◆ At times we may be beset by feelings of inadequacy, bondage, limitation, and frustration. These attitudes of mind, unless changed, may lead to a distrust in ourselves. We may say we are not up to the daily routine or tasks of living, and this mental attitude may make even the *simplest* of activities seem almost *insurmountable*. Fear, frustration, and insecurity cause us to feel separated from life. We may feel we are completely *on our own* and through our individual efforts must *fight* to acquire and maintain the good things of life. Competition in business, friendships, and even in family relationships, follows the unhealthy feeling that we must struggle to hold our own or surpass the other fellow. This false concept of competition and its many attending ills, we may be sure, is always the result of thinking of ourself as being completely separated from life and on our own. Our intellect tells us we *cannot live unto ourself alone,* yet how often are we impelled by experience to feel that we must do so. This attitude of "being on the fence" may lead to a complete disbelief in ourselves unless something is done to change it. The answer lies in the larger vision of our true selves and our relationship to others and to God. We can begin by saying, "I and all other persons exist in the one life because God is life. We come from God and are one with God. Our soul is one with the soul of the Universe, or God. Our Spirit is one with the Infinite Spirit, or knowingness of God. All that we are is God, *as us.* This is true of all persons." As we inwardly accept this truth, we feel, within, the security of a reserve of power and wisdom to be called upon in times of seeming loneliness and need.

ð¶ My soul is *secure,* because I did not create it. I am one with the soul-side of life, or God. God expresses through me now and always as Infinite Wisdom. I sense this oneness with God in all persons. In my business dealings, I draw upon the reservoir of wisdom within me to make *correct decisions* for my good and the good of all concerned. Because I believe in my oneness with God, I can turn to God in any situation and receive guidance and help. I am not disturbed by appearances. I am not anxious, nor do I entertain doubts as to my abilities. In and through all my contacts with life, I am sustained in the knowledge that I am one with God in whom all people live, move, and have their being. Knowing this, I cannot help but believe in myself, the Real self, the Divine self.

MY DESTINY IS SECURE—FOR I AM ONE WITH GOD

> *"The wise shall inherit glory, but shame shall be the promotion of fools."*
>
> *–Proverbs 3:35*

Infinite Spirit within me, as me, sets the course of my life.

ð¶ Often we make ourselves unhappy by too much *doubtful introspection.* We try to work everything out ahead of time or feel frustrated because we do not know all the answers to all things. This attitude stems from a subtle distrust in the self, which is in reality *a distrust in God.* When we have the feeling of complete oneness with our creator, we are filled with warmth of courage, security and love, regardless of external appearances. Sometimes the happiest moment in our life will be when we can say that we don't know the answer to all questions; that we don't have to know what will happen the next moment, next month, or next year. What we do know is, "I am one with God—God is good." Our destiny is linked with the *basic integrity* of the Universe. Even though we may doubt and make wrong decisions that temporarily lead to undesirable experiences, we can be assured that, in the overall scheme of things, all is well with us, for God cannot be wrong.

&. This day I am filled with *courage* and a sense of *well-being*, for I know my destiny is secure. This security is guaranteed through my recognition of my oneness with God. My destiny as a divine child of the Most High is that I shall express myself. I realize that the "myself" that knows, plans, and sets the pattern of my experiences from day to day is the Spirit of God expressing through me, as me. I know my experience of living is not *blueprinted* or *predestined*. Through my partnership with Infinite Spirit, my daily experiences and my future destiny are created as I sense Its guidance. As I believe in God and myself, I know my destiny is secure. I open my mind to the *inspiration*, *guidance*, and *love* of the Divine Presence. Even though I do not know all the answers with my intellect, faith dispels all fear, doubt, and uncertainty. I move from moment to moment in *joyous expectancy*, knowing my destiny is secure.

MY LIFE IS THE LIFE OF GOD—IT IS GOOD

"Knew ye not that ye are the temple of God, and that the Spirit of God dwelleth in you."
—I Corinthians 3:16

am one with God-life, the potential of all I desire.

&. Should we find that we are *too tense* in the business of living; strenuously forcing ourselves to make decisions—willing ourselves to be friendly or others to like us—being concerned with how our feelings are "feeling" today—chances are that we are taking on a *false sense* of responsibility. Not that we do not have responsibility, but it would seem that one's sacred duty is to be true to oneself, one's real inner self. God imposes the edict that we shall discover ourselves, become increasingly aware of the potentialities that lie within us. If this process of *self-discovery* is based on the knowledge of the unity of all life, and that life is the life of God, living takes on a new meaning. Morbid self-concern disappears as we realize we did not *create* life—*we use it*. It is God-life as our life that we express. New insight comes with the understanding that we are all God-beings, using, experiencing, and expressing the same life that is our life. To make our life one of ease rather than disease, one of happiness and more inclusive of the all-good, we must feel that the good we desire for ourself we would desire for all people. In return, we should know that others would desire for us only the best that life has to offer. *Strenuous living* based on separation, jealousy, envy, and selfish desires, *disappears* with this larger vision.

᪣ Today—this moment—I thrill to the heartbeat of the Infinite Presence within me. This life is the eternal life of God, proclaiming itself through me, as me. As thoughts of separation, anxiety, or past unhappy experiences try to assert themselves, I have but to turn within, *recognize* and *thank* God for Its presence within me. I am now lifted out of any sense of false responsibility regarding my life or the lives of others. I know at this instant from the center of my being, God-good moves out through my every act, thought, and word. This life activity is Infinite Wisdom in action. Harmony, peace of mind, flood my being as I gratefully acknowledge the Presence of God life as my life now. All that I desire moves into my experience through *any needed channel*. I am the way through which life moves and the way through which God pours Its bounty, to me and through me, blessing all whom I contact. This day, and every day, I am aware that only good goes from me and only good returns to me.

GOD-LIFE IS MY LIFE NOW

> *"For as the Father hath life in himself, so hath he*
> *given to the Son to have life in himself."*
>
> *—John 5:26*

*T*here is one life, God-life. This life is my life now, not at sometime in the *past*, not at some future time, but right *now* is the Eternal Life of God manifesting in me and through me, as me.

᪣ I know that my life is the spirit of God in action. The spirit of life within me is all-wise and sustains me in every way. I am conscious of the *vitality* and *strength* of God-life *sustaining* me always. As I realize this to be true, I let go of everything within my thinking that says I can be separated from the One Life, and I feel the energizing vitality and strength of the Infinite Presence flood my entire body. The activity of God-Spirit as God-Life, created my body. My body is a manifestation or expression of the Divine idea of body within the Mind of God. Regardless of any appearance, I know nothing has ever happened to this spiritual idea. It is perfect. As I think in terms of my oneness with the wholeness of life, God-life, this becomes my experience.

ཡ་ At this moment, I accept, in faith, that the Life-force within me *knows what to do* to sustain and maintain Itself. I do not struggle, or with my *intellect*, try to force or will the Life within me to express Itself. I know it is Its nature to express, and as It is the activity of God-spirit, I know that It knows how to express perfectly. At this moment, I cease to give undue importance or reality to any apparent lack of vitality or strength. I turn my *attention in blessing* to my God-perfection. I steadfastly hold to this image that God must have for me as one of God's beloved children. By keeping my thoughts affirmative and vitally positive, I cooperate with Infinite Spirit and let It *direct every bodily activity*. That which would appear to hinder or limit the functioning of the God-Life through me is rendered powerless as I feel my Oneness with Perfect Life—the Life of God.

PAST MISTAKES DO NOT AFFECT ME

> *"...but this one thing I do, forgetting those things which are behind, and reaching unto those things which are before, I press toward the mark for the prize of the high calling of God."*
>
> *—Philippians 3:13,14*

*T*oday I *forgive myself* of all past mistakes, for I realize that *today* is the only day I shall ever experience. "Now is the accepted time."

ཡ་ As I realize my God-intended privilege of self-choice, I know that with it goes the ability to makes mistakes. I recognize any past so-called mistakes only as *less desirable* or unwise choices. They are not things of themselves and have power only through my conscious or unconscious acceptance of them. This day, the word that I speak has the power to eliminate the effect of any past mistake as I realize that *God does not condemn* but, through *God's love,* has given me freedom to accept that which I choose. If God does not condemn, neither do I, and any sense of self-condemnation is immediately neutralized as I turn from the past and know that as I think and accept *now,* so shall it be. I *forgive myself* for any past unwise choice by ceasing to give it power to make me unhappy. Today, I shall do better. *I forgive others* for any past real, or imagined cause of hurt in my life. Through understanding and *love,* the power of any hurt to make me unhappy, from whatever source, is removed. Complete forgiveness comes through my recognition, now, of the Presence of Infinite Wisdom within me, responding to me as I now turn to It.

ᘒ This day I allow only that which is *constructive,* either from the past or the anticipated future. to occupy my thought. Any thought of condemnation or past mistake is instantly neutralized as the Spirit of love and understanding flows through me. Serenity of mind and persistency of purpose fill my entire being as I embody a willingness to let only good flow from me. In this awareness, I know only good can return to me. In *joyous expectancy* and *gratitude,* I accept my good now.

I AM A DIVINE INDIVIDUAL

> *"Behold what manner of love the Father hath
> bestowed upon us, that we should be called the sons
> of God....Beloved, now are we the sons of God...."*
> *–I John 3:1,2*

As I look upon the outer experiences taking place in my life, I realize, in Truth, that they are all some part of me. They are but outwardly expressing that which I have inwardly accepted. As I turn within myself, in thought, I am aware that all that I am is *rooted* in a Presence and a Power, the full nature of which is beyond my intellect to understand. But this I do know—that this Presence moves through me, as me, and as it does, I am expressing, in a very real manner, my Divine individuality. As I accept this truth and have a *willingness* to increasingly become an unobstructed way through which the nature of Infinite Spirit expresses, I create in my outer experiences peace, harmony, and good. In this way, the outer reflects the inner. The experience and the experiencer are one.

Because I am constantly expressing life, I am constantly experiencing more of my Divine individuality. This day I recognize the high responsibility and the great privilege of being the *way* through which God-Mind works. While I enter into life in its objective expression, there is the assurance that as the experiencer I may assume dominion over all that I experience. This dominion is asserted lovingly and understandingly, and I realize that this is only possible because I am a Divine individual, "a dispenser of the Divine gifts."

Even though I positively assert my own individuality, there is no feeling of separation from others. As I realize that each is a "Child of the Most High," I experience a deep respect and understanding, of and for the individuality of every other person.

   As I increasingly become aware that I am inwardly one with the harmony and beauty of the One Life, so do the outer phases of my life increasingly *reflect* the *harmony*, *beauty*, and the *good* of God-Mind, which expresses through me, as me. This day and every day, I constantly remind myself of my Divine source, that I am a Divine being, yet one with the whole of Life. As I persist in this high image of myself and others, I am sustained and blessed in all that I do. Truly in my experience I behold the generous *outpouring of love* that only the Father can bestow upon his child. As I reflect this love in word, thought, and deed, all whom I contact are blessed.

I EXPRESS MY GOD-INTENDED FREEDOM WISELY

> *"And ye shall know the truth, and the truth shall make you free."*
>
> *—John 8:32*

Freedom is something that must be cherished and appreciated. By the *grace of God*, this *unearned gift* has been made, and by this same grace have we been given the *intelligence* to understand, guard, and wisely use our freedom. We must accept and nourish the divine gift of thoughtfulness, love, and wisdom. Within the very gift of freedom are the seeds of *relative* bondage. It is true that "all men are created equal"—equal in that each one is endowed potentially with all wisdom, power, and the opportunity for self-expression. In the eyes of God not only "are all alive, "but each is a "child of the Most High." It is in the unwise use of this divine birthright that hurtful bondage is created. We are often bound by our use of freedom. The Law of Cause and Effect, stimulated by our freedom of choice, is the law that "binds the ignorant, but frees the wise."

Truly, we must guard our freedom with all our heart and mind. It is helpful to recognize our oneness with all of life and with all people. Perceiving the divinity of every other person, we are prompted to act wisely, thoughtfully, and lovingly in our relationship with others. Where this divinity of others is recognized and respected, there could be no hurtful bondage in our day-to-day experience; not to have this feeling of *empathy* could set up a sense of separation from life and bring hurt into our lives. We must also expect and know that others will respect our divine heritage. This is using our God-intended freedom wisely (constructively and free from hurt), and the only bondage that can possibly result is a bondage with the whole of life, under the *law of love*.

    Today I express my Divinity in understanding and love. I recognize and respect the true God-self in all persons whom I contact this day. There is no thought in my mind of coercion or desire to hurt another in any way; therefore in *joyous expectancy* I know I will experience harmony, respect, and love wherever I go and in whatever I do. My word is powerful in *awakening* the Divinity within me and in all whom I contact.

In my life, and in the lives of all humanity, I sense the Presence of Infinite Spirit proclaiming God-intended freedom, under the only bondage that is real—that of love, unity, and wholeness.

MY SUCCESS IS ASSURED

> *"And he that reapeth receiveth wages, and gathereth fruit unto life eternal, that both he that soweth, and he that reapeth, may rejoice together."*
>
> *–John 4:36*

In God there are no failures. Today, I realize my unity with God and know there can really be no failure in my life. It is true that through negative comparison of myself and my status in life, with others whom I have thought of as being successful, I may have built up a *belief* in my own inability to accomplish. This I have *interpreted* as failure. I now declare that any thought of failure, past or present, is ineffective in my experience. As I see success in others, I truly rejoice with them and mentally enter into the happiness their good brings to them. God within me, as me, succeeds in everything that I do. Success to me means self-expression in such a way that others may be benefited. I find something in that which I am *now doing* that meets this need. Thus, I build a consciousness of success.

I realize that my endeavors express my God-intended individuality. That which I do is appreciated by those whom I serve. As my consciousness expands, an awareness of my greater potential is realized, and my opportunity for service for and to others is increased. Under the law of *compensation*, I am justly recompensed for all that I do. Thus the fruits of my success are increased.

❧ Today, I let go of any past thought-patterns of limitation. Now, at this moment, the Spirit of God that can know no failure, moves through me in all I think, do, and say, bringing greater opportunities into my life. I *let go* of prejudice, dogmatic opinion, past negative experience, and let Spirit move through me, as me, into paths of action that assure me of continued success. How wonderful to realize that as *I give of myself* in helpfulness and service to others, I am *making room* for an ever-increasing good to move into my life. This is the blessing of life. It cannot fail.

I ENVY NO ONE

"Be kindly affectioned one to another...in honour preferring one another."

–*Romans 12:10*

Regardless of how long I may have entertained thoughts of envy, I now eliminate them from my mind. I now realize that by being jealous or envious of others, I am really condemning myself. The effects of such thinking are removed as I come to understand that every time I envy another's good fortune, I am literally impressing upon my mind that I, myself, *do not possess* good; and that which I believe or feel to be true about myself is that which I experience.

Therefore, this day I rise above any feeling that anyone may be envious of me or that I may be envious of another. By knowing that each is heir to the kingdom and each is experiencing according to his acceptance of the Divine gifts, I *rejoice* in the good that others experience. This rejoicing is akin to *love*, and as I wholeheartedly enter into it, I open the way for a greater good to come into my life.

ã€€ This day I am positive in my *refusal to believe* that anyone is envious of me, and I declare that no thought of jealousy toward another can enter my consciousness. I am aware of the presence and the availability of all good things, and rejoice in the good experienced by others. This knowledge opens a new future for me and I experience and express increased understanding and love.

As I persist in an affirmative *self-image of worthiness* as a Divine being and calmly sense Divine ideas motivating my every thought and act, I enter each day with an expectancy of good.

HARMONY EXPRESSES IN MY HOME

"The Spirit itself beareth witness with our spirit, that we are the children of God."

–Romans 8:16

I recognize the presence of God-spirit in my home, expressing through every member of my household. Each person in my home is a Divine individual. I respect the individuality of each one and in turn know that each understands and respects the individuality of the other.

The Presence and the Power of Spirit, which is All-wise, knows what to do to maintain *love* and *true understanding* in all the activities and deliberations that take place in my home. At all times, thoughtfulness, respect, love, and understanding permit freedom of expression according to the law of Divine Harmony and Oneness. The Presence and Power maintains right action in all *necessary adjustments*. There is a closeness of understanding love that sustains each with a feeling of support and well-being. Joy and happiness dominate as we sense *we are loved* and as each expresses understanding love in all ways. In this understanding love, each for the other, all in my home feel their rightful importance. Deliberations and councils are always inspired by consideration and the highest of motives. Egotism, jealousy, or hurt cannot exist, for they have nothing upon which to feed. All members of my home are impelled to act, think, and express themselves in such a way as to eliminate any feeling of frustration or condemnation of self or others.

ã€€ An atmosphere of harmony and a unity of purpose, plan, and action now pervades my home and blesses each member with Divine inspiration for a richer expression of his God-intended self. The *healing atmosphere* of harmony and love sustains and blesses our home and all who pass our way.

TODAY I ACCEPT ABUNDANCE

"Blessed is that man that maketh the Lord his trust."

—*Psalms 40:4*

*T*o God there is no "great nor small." God the absolute could not be conscious of relative big or little, limitation or abundance. As an individual expressing objectively, I am conscious of the relative experiences of life. I recognize that any experience of limitation is not a thing of itself, but rather a limited use or expression of the Infinite potential of all good. Knowing this, I bless the good that I have and this blessing now sows the seeds for the greater good to come into my experience.

From this moment, I release any sense of the *necessity* of limitation. My acceptance of any desired good is established as I *release* any feeling of tension or strain in connection with the *apparent lack*. It is the Father's good pleasure to give me that which is of the kingdom of God—good.

That which I desire embodies only *right action* for all concerned. It provides an expanded self-expression and opens the way for me to give increasingly of myself. All persons connected with my desire are benefited. The law of harmony, beauty, and self-expression—God's law of right action—assures me of my success. I experience abounding opportunity for self-expression.

❧ Spirit knows, right now, what I should do, say, and think. As I accept this realization, in faith, and *inwardly listen* expectantly, it is as though the Presence of God takes me by the hand and leads me, gently and lovingly, into paths of accomplishment. I have a willingness to believe that I am being led, guided, and directed. I will do what I must do. I let go of old limiting thought patterns, dismissing them with love and blessings. I welcome my new experience with *courage, faith*, and *trust*. Today I accept my greater good. As I speak my word of affirmation, all that is necessary for its complete fulfillment is now in operation, moving toward me as I move toward it.

I APPRECIATE MY DIVINITY

"And if children, then heirs: heirs of God...."
–Romans 8:18

$\mathcal{G}$od created the human being in God's own image and likeness. Realizing this *close relationship* between the Infinite and myself, I free my thought from any self-condemnation or self-depreciation. To continue in such morbid attitudes of mind would be to *dishonor* my Divine heritage. Therefore, I accept the responsibility entailed in being a child of the Most High.

"I and my Creator are one." As I realize the full implication of this relationship, I know that within me at any time and under any circumstance, Infinite Spirit stands ready to assist, guide, and direct. *I am never alone.*

As I accept my image as a Divine individual, I fully appreciate my worth, effectiveness, and usefulness to others. My acceptance of myself as worthy opens the doorway of opportunity that the Infinite may increasingly flow through me, bringing good to me and all whom I contact. There is no thought of egotism as I praise the God qualities potentially within me, for I know that *all others* are also children of the Most High. All contribute to my well-being as I *consciously* seek to assist others. I am never alone.

❧ This day I know I am open and receptive to greater good, richer opportunities, and Divine Guidance, as I embrace a fuller concept of my true worth as a Divine being. As I recognize in others their worth, all barriers of resistance, competition, and separation are dissolved. In my world of conditions and affairs, all things are working together for good. All whom I contact are blessed, even as I am blessed, as I appreciate and express my Divinity.

INNER TRANQUILITY REMOVES ALL FEAR

*"Fear not, little flock; for it is your Father's good
pleasure to give you the kingdom."*

–*Luke 12:32*

*T*oday is the *eternal day* of my experience. I do not deny the past as experience, but I affirm that I cannot live in the past except as a *memory* of what has happened. It is also true that I cannot live in the future, but my anticipation of the future can affect this present moment of my thinking.

My mental and emotional reaction at any given moment *sets the tone* of my experience of this moment. Therefore I now affirm that any fear or uncertainty that I may have had in the past, may assert itself at this time only if today I am either consciously or unconsciously giving it that power. At this moment, this same ability of acceptance enables me to turn from any fear and embrace only feelings of confidence and security.

Through my realization of the Presence of the One Spirit—the Power of God in all things—I know there is a *basic integrity* in the Universe. This integrity is purpose, balance, harmony, and *love*. This integrity I now affirm as the Divine impulsion of the sustaining love of God within me.

As I turn from fear, regardless of what its cause may have been, I make room for the Divine nature, the peace and harmony of action, to move into my thought and life. As I accept and feel this Presence and Power flowing through me and my experience, I know this to be true about all persons. I see the integrity of God moving through *all things* and *all persons*. As I understand my Oneness with God, any fear of life or other people and of myself is dissolved.

& Today, I consciously let go of my fears and let understanding, *love*, and faith *direct* me in all things. I imagine myself as being in the midst of and surrounded by Divine right action, and I know the support of the integrity of God-life and Being always upholds me. I move easily and serenely with complete freedom from anxiety or fear.

MY HEART SINGS IN PERFECT RHYTHM

"Cast away from you all your transgressions...and make you a new heart...."

–Ezekiel 18:31

*T*oday, this moment, I let my heart beat in perfect rhythm. I do not *make* it do this; I accept that my heart expresses that action for which God in His Infinite Wisdom created it. There is a perfect *idea* of heart in the Mind of God. This idea neither I nor anyone else created. Nothing has ever happened to this perfect idea. My heart is expressing this God-idea right now.

Whatever may have taken place in my experience to lead to feelings of anxiety and separation from life, I know need no longer affect me in any way. My heart is a symbol of *love* and *understanding* that goes out from me to all persons. I approve of myself and forgive myself any unwise choice or past mistake or action. As I move out in love toward others and life itself, the circle of harmony is complete, and I meet the approval of others and of life making itself felt in all that I do. The harmony and rhythm of God-Life pours Itself through me as vital circulation and elimination of anything that does not belong. I am not anxious, for I *trust* the Wisdom and Presence of God-Life to sustain and *recreate* that which it has created.

I feel strength and vitality in every heartbeat. I do not listen for it, I am not anxious about it; for I accept now that God-Intelligence, God-Life knows what to do to maintain perfect heart action and circulation.

🙠 I now free my mind from any jealousy, envy, hatred, or malice. I make room for joy, happiness, and a sense of well-being to possess me. I bless my body and my heart. This blessing becomes real as I extend it to life and all whom I meet from day to day.

I know this *constructive* and *affirmative* word has the power to remove any physical or mental obstruction, and my mind is now open for complete guidance in allowing my heart to sing in perfect rhythm.

PEACE OF MIND SUSTAINS ME AT ALL TIMES

"He that dwelleth in the secret place of the Most High shall abide under the shadow of the Almighty."

–Psalms 91:1

At the center of my being is the *quiet Mind*, the Mind of God. It is here that I realize my Oneness with all creation, for here is the kingdom of God. From this center of God-consciousness, all things proceed. Should I become confused by passing events or by things that my intellect does not fully comprehend, I find immediate calm as I *turn within* to that place of harmony and balance that can know nothing of confusion. In this "secret place of the Most High" dwells the Divine self, the Real me. I am never separated from this Real self, no matter what seems to be taking place in my experience. I now know that my experience is but a passing event, the seeds of which have been sown through my conscious or unconscious acceptance. Realizing this, the experience loses its importance as a "thing of itself," with power to confuse or upset me. Behind all experience is the experiencer. This is that within me which knows and comprehends. In my individual life, without this experiencer there would be no experience. Behind that within me which knows, there is the Infinite Knower, without which there would be no experiencer or experience. This Infinite Knower is never confused, frustrated, or upset.

I allow peace to replace confusion in my mind, body, and affairs, not by denial of the experience but by understanding it and looking through it to that place within which is *never disturbed*. Conditions cannot control me or confuse me, for being consciously One with Spirit, I can assume dominion over my life and affairs. I do this by letting go of the feeling that I must use will power or force to establish peace of mind and by letting the peace of God, at the center of my mind, take possession.

ea At this moment, I turn in confidence from confusion to the Presence of the All-knowing Spirit within me. It floods my awareness with its Presence. I have faith now, and at all times, to know that *Infinite Spirit moves through me, as me*, to establish and maintain peace of mind. I rest secure as I know that Infinite harmony and peace accompanies and enters into every activity of my life.

RESTFUL SLEEP IS MINE

"I will both lay me down in peace, and sleep: for thou, Lord, only makest me dwell in safety."
–Psalms 4:8

As I retire for the night, restful sleep envelops me. I consciously let slip from my mind any problems that may have presented themselves during the day. I also release from conscious attention any contemplated action for tomorrow. I realize that the past and that which is to happen in the future are the results of states of mind. So also is the *present moment* a state of mind.

Right now, I do not force or will myself to sleep. Sleep is the normal experience of the relaxing, revitalizing and harmonizing of every aspect of my being. Sleep follows naturally the letting go of any sense of force, tension, or anxiety. My will or desire becomes a willingness to let the God-intended function of sleep possess me. As I accept this, the Life Principle, or God as instinctive life, takes over the functions of my mind and body. I am willing to let this be so.

Sleep envelops me as I quietly resolve, now, to intellectually let go and "let God" *take over for the next few hours.* God within me guides and directs all bodily functions. I let go of any anxious thought for tomorrow, knowing God will guide and direct me and all concerned in the activities of the days to come. There will be only right action.

❧ This confidence of Divine support and guidance instills within me, now, the realization that I can completely, and without reservation, place my affairs in the hands of the Infinite Presence. In complete faith I let my mind and body become enfolded in restful sleep, knowing that I will awake in the morning, renewed in body and refreshed in mind. Restful sleep is mine now.

I MAKE CORRECT DECISIONS

"But rather seek ye the kingdom of God, and all
these things shall be added unto you."

–Luke 12:31

*T*oday any apparent indecision has no power to make me unhappy or confused. I realize that in making any decision it is not necessary that I know *all* of the answers or actions involved in what is to follow. I can now determine that I don't have to decide on every issue in connection with my particular need. I now assume this positive attitude of mind.

Whatever is to happen as a result of my decision I know will mean a larger expression of life for me and it will bring good to all persons involved. My decision, *right now*, is to know that Infinite Spirit within me knows, step by step, how to bring this good about. Right now, being All-wise, It knows just what decision is to be made and when. Infinite Spirit, being everywhere present, right now knows through what *channels* my good shall come and guides and directs all concerned. As in faith I accept this to be true, there is an inner assurance that only right action can prevail and only good can come to me and all concerned.

I do not hesitate to admit that my intellect is quite limited in its capacity to know all the answers in connection with my problem or need for adjustment. Any sense of anxiety is removed and faith is established as I now know my intellect, or my spiritual quality of self-knowingness can and does *permit* God-wisdom to guide and direct in any specific need.

❧ My *decision*, right now, is to free my mind from anxiety and to know that I shall be *impelled* to act, think, and decide in the right way and at the right time. I am alert to the presence of Spirit within me, moving through me, as me, to make the correct decision at the right time. I move toward my desired good with a sense of ease, confidence, and joyous *expectancy*.

GOD-LIFE WITHIN ME IS FREE FROM ILLNESS

*"Thy word have I hid in mine heart, that I might
not sin against thee."*

—Psalms 119:11

God-life within me is the *presence* and *activity* of Spirit. Freed
from any superstitious belief about punishment in the form of disease.
I now fearlessly look at and understand the experience, be it pain,
inflammation or congestion. I understand this experience is never a
thing of and by itself, but is always the result of an acceptance that is
sustained by an inward belief.

My word, which I now speak, is a *new* and *positive belief*, and I am
the believer. As I remove a sense of fear and anxiety from my problem,
its importance is lessened in my mind. I know that pain or any disease
in only a signal or *reminder* that there is an obstruction to the perfect
functioning of God-life as my body. Knowing this, my negative
attitude of fear or confusion is replaced by an affirmative feeling of
gratitude for the *signal* telling me that something needs to be done.

I now know that right where this condition of congestion, irritation, or pain is, there is the Intelligence of God-life active as my life,
now. This word that I speak is the word of Spirit expressing through
me as my word, now. I turn from the condition and allow vitality,
adjustment, and harmony to express.

❧ I realize this word of itself does not make the necessary adjustment
or remove pain, congestion, and inflammation. But as I contemplate
the truth of its meaning, it establishes my willingness to be freed from
frustrations, fears, and confusion of mind and permits Spirit *automatically* to establish wholeness in me.

Peace of mind and body is mine, now, as I realize that God-life is
my life, and my life is the activity of the wisdom and *love* of Spirit
maintaining peaceful, vital, and harmonious action throughout my
body.

DIVINE GUIDANCE ANSWERS MY EVERY NEED

"I will instruct thee, and teach thee in the way which thou shalt go."

–Psalms 32:8

f I seem to be at a loss as to *how* to proceed when a need for action or direction arises in my experience, I realize *I am never alone.* "The Father and I are one." All of my requests under the great law of life are honored by the God Principle within me. The affirmative nature of God always says yes to my *inward* desires. Because I cannot, with my intellect, perceive the answers to any particular need at any given time, does not mean that God has deserted me.

God does for me what I *allow* Him to do. Therefore, this day I cease to struggle with my problem. I let Infinite Spirit move through me in my need at this moment. I do not tell God *how* to respond to my need, nor *how* to lead me, but rather turn in faith and quiet confidence to the Presence within. I remove all negative opinions and beliefs in order to make room for the acceptance of Divine Guidance.

Right now I know the Spirit within knows what to do through me in my particular need. Only right action for myself and all others involved can prevail. What I am impelled to do brings into my life a richer experience and a greater opportunity for *self-expression.*

&. Today, I release any sense of anxiety. I accept in faith, and I know and feel that God honors my request for Divine Guidance, by *knowing through me,* as me, that which I should do and know. I listen quietly and move vitally and enthusiastically in the direction in which I am led. I am guided, sustained, and directed by Infinite Wisdom in my every need.

TODYA I HAVE ALL THE VITALITY I NEED

"Fear thou not; for I am with thee; be not dismayed,
for I am thy God; I will strengthen thee...."

–Isaiah 41:10

*M*y vitality is the activity of God-life within me. As God-life is limitless and cannot be exhausted, so I know my vitality cannot, actually, be exhausted. Any *belief* that I have so much strength to *use* and when that is gone I shall be fatigued, is now cleared from my consciousness.

I am aware at this moment that I am one with all vitality. At the center of my being, there is the *potential* of all strength for anything that I undertake. As I now realize that I am a Divine being expressing my Divine-self in service to humanity, there is no friction, frustration, or sense of drudgery in that which I do. I am interested in life and people. I love life and people, even as I love my true self. I move along with life from experience to experience. Each moment I meet with joyous expectancy. I do not resist or struggle, resent or worry. As I release the necessity of these frictions from my thinking, strength moves in me and through me.

Today my life is *orderly* and freed from frustrating doubt. I move from moment to moment *joyously.* I am constantly buoyed up and strengthened in all that I do. The harmony and balanced action of Spirit within me is the vitality of God within me, now. Today I have all the vitality I need, as I *wisely* and affirmatively use God's gift of life to me.

MY BODY IS A DIVINE IDEA

*"... know ye not that your body is the temple of the
Holy Ghost which is in you."*
                                              –I Corinthians 6:19

*T*his day and every day I bless my body for being the wonderful
instrument that it is. The *substance* of my body is the Divine substance
of God. The *form* of my body is patterned after the Divine idea of body
in the Mind of God. I release from my thought any sense of condemnation or lack of appreciation for my body. It is a Divine idea, and as
such I am completely grateful for it. I did not create my body, I do not
create the intelligent life action that sustains it. I realize, now, that
nothing in Reality has ever happened to this *Divine* idea in the mind
of God, the creator and sustainer. I know that any appearance of
disease need not be. It has no reality in Truth other than that which
I give it but is a manifestation of a belief of negative ideas I have either
consciously or unconsciously accepted. In spite of any appearance, I
know that instinctive life within me is the activity of Spirit; its nature
is harmony, balance, and right action, expressing as the Law of my
being. This Life-principle within me now knows what to do and how
to *maintain* and *sustain* my body in complete wholeness.

I open my mind to a greater insight and spiritual awareness and
know that Spirit, the All-Wise, knows what to do to establish and
maintain wholeness, harmony, and balance in every *bodily function*
within me. There is a willingness on my part now, in spite of any
preconceived opinion or belief, to let Spirit as Perfect Life carry out
its purpose. My acceptance of this truth removes any obstruction that
has been placed in the way of God's idea from expressing through me.
My body is a Divine idea. I respect it. I bless it, for it is the temple of
the living Spirit of God within me, as me.

THIS DAY IS A NEW BEGINNING

> *"Jesus Christ the same yesterday, and today, and forever."*
>
> *–Hebrews 13:8*

*T*his day is a new beginning. As I move into the activities of this day, I declare that *new adventures* in living await me at every turn. Unpleasant experiences of my yesterdays have power to make me unhappy and anxious only to the extent that I permit them to be a part of this day's awareness.

Today my mind is filled with glorious *anticipation*. No problem arises that cannot be worked out harmoniously. There is no anxiety that can enter my thought, for I deeply feel my true relationship with life. My desires for this day are governed only by right action. Only good for myself and all who enter into my day's activity *motivates* my thoughts and actions.

Infinite Spirit through the Law of God-mind goes before and paves the way for me. Spirit speaks through me in all that I say. Wisdom governs all that I do. Regardless of any past experience, or how much it may try to impinge on my consciousness today, it is now rendered ineffective.

In calmness and with complete reliance upon Spirit to guide and direct me in every need, all sense of frustration and anxiety disappears. Serenity possesses me as I realize that there is an *integrity* to life and *God is for me*. Courage and a sense of well-being envelop me as I find self-approval through an affirmative understanding of my God-self. I accept that which is desirable from the past and joyfully anticipate the good that is to come into my experience. I enjoy the good that today offers. This day, this moment, is a new beginning.

MY BUSINESS IS CONSUMMATED

"Let all things be done decently, and in order."
                                              –I Corinthians 14:40

This possession that I have, I now desire to sell. Whether it be a house, automobile, furniture, or any other good thing, I desire to pass it along to someone else to enjoy. I bless it for the good that I have received through my *use* of it. The good experienced provides the pattern through which an ever *greater good* comes to me as I make room for it. I know that as I completely release that which I desire to sell, the good I have derived through possessing it will be passed along to someone else for their *enjoyment*.

There is a willingness on my part, now, to completely let go of any sense of personal possession or *holding on*, through happy memories or associations, to that which I wish to sell. I completely release it, knowing that under the law of circulation of life action and the law of growth, a greater good automatically moves in to take its place. This transaction embodies only right action and good for all concerned. There is in it no element of hurt, and each is benefited. All are Divinely guided as to price, terms, and conditions under which the sale takes place.

❧ Infinite Spirit knows right now who wants that which I have to sell. I am led to know, and *do* all things necessary to bring this to the attention of the right person or persons. Infinite Intelligence now does whatever It should to lead that person or persons to me who want that which I now lovingly and completely release from my possession. To God-mind this already is a *completed transaction*.

The sale that I wish to make is consummated.

MY WORK IS A THING OF JOY

"And there are diversities of operations, but it is the same God which worketh all in all."

–I Corinthians 12:6

*T*he nature of God is self-expression, a giving of Itself to creation. So it logically follows that our human nature must be to give of ourselves. That which I do cannot have any semblance of drudgery connected with it, as I now see it as the way through which I express my Divine nature of *self-giving that others may be helped.*

As I look for that helpfulness to others in my work and find it, I realize that I am expressing my Divine birthright, and I am filled with a sense of well-being. As I release from my mind any sense of compulsion or drudgery in what I do, I act with increased ease and efficiency. I become an ever-increasing channel through which good, helpfulness, and service flows to others.

I am not satisfied to stand still in my mode of self-expression, neither am I overawed by a feeling of Divine discontent ever urging me on to new desires and experiences. Spirit within me knows how I can serve best according to my talents at this present time. I am never required to do anything that I cannot do successfully. If some aspects of my work seem less enjoyable than others, I am not discontented. I always give the best that I have in any endeavor.

ex Guided by Infinite Spirit, I am constantly aware of greater possibilities for self-expression. My talents are appreciated by all whom I serve. I am justly and abundantly compensated in all that I do. Happiness comes to me as I realize that through service, the giving of myself in *love*, others are helped and made happy.

My work is an adventure from day to day. This day my work is a thing of joy.

I AM RENEWED IN BODY AND MIND EACH DAY

"Who satisfieth thy mouth with good things; so that thy youth is renewed like the eagles."

–Psalms 103:5

In my thinking there is no problem of growing old or of old age. Chronological time is but the measurement of *a series of events* taking place in the eternal ever-present now. My life is the expression of the eternal Life of God. My spirit is the Spirit of God-Eternal as me. My soul is the *individualized* expression of the Universal Over-Soul of God Being. My body is the substance of God as definite form. Therefore, the *real me* knows nothing about exhausting itself or growing old. There is within me at this moment all the Power and Presence of God. It sustains and maintains me as a perfect and harmonious expression of life. In faith, I consciously turn to this sustaining Presence within me, knowing I am renewed in mind and body.

As I embody this greater awareness of my true state of being, any problem of growing old disappears. I move harmoniously from experience to experience as I realize that God-life moves in and through me as my life, always. I do not dwell unduly on previous happy experiences with a desire to relive them in the present. Each day, while it may be colored by the past, becomes a new and glorious experience, as I realize the presence of the Eternal Spirit that sustains me always.

❧ I now free my thought of any anxieties regarding the future and remove all negative comparisons with the past. I let the joyous, happy, and profitable past experience move into the present as the foundation greater acceptance of good. I am now renewed in body and mind as I, with joyous anticipation, enter the activities of this eternal day.

I CONSISTENTLY USE GOD LAW

"No man having put his hand to the plough, and looking back, is fit for the kingdom of God."

–Luke 9:62

Regardless of what the undesirable situation or condition may be or how long it has existed, I know it can be *changed*. Without blame or evasion, I accept the fact that, through my God-intended power of choice, I have either consciously or unconsciously permitted the undesirable experience to take place.

The very Law of Mind by which the experience was created is the same God-law that I now use to bring about the desired change. The word that I now speak is the law of elimination of the undesirable and at the same time the way through which my right desire comes into being.

I am not dismayed if my good is not *instantly* produced, although I place no time limit on my demonstration. I am earnest and sincere in my endeavor to know the truth about my particular need. Spirit moves through me, doing what It should to pave the way for my complete acceptance of my good. My affirmative *persistence* permits my greater awareness of the presence and power of Spirit to respond constructively according to my need.

According to my acceptance and belief is it done unto me.

❧ The word that I now speak and every future word that I may speak, continues to be the way through which any undesirable past thought patterns are rendered ineffective. My word is the Law unto that whereunto it is spoken. Steadfast in my acceptance and freed from anxiety or force of will, I permit the good that I desire to move into my life easily, harmoniously, and completely. With joyous expectancy, I let the Law of God—Good—be made manifest through me now.

THROUGH GIVING, I BLESS MYSELF AND OTHERS

"Cast thy bread upon the waters: for thou shalt find it after many days."

–Ecclesiastes 11:1

This day, and every day, I seek ways in which to give of myself that others may be helped. While it is "more blessed to give than to receive," I also realize that under the Law of attraction, unfoldment, and growth, "the gift is greatest to the giver." Realizing the oneness of all life, *I give freely to others*, knowing that as I do I am not only helping others, but, in reality, am actually giving to some other aspect of myself. That which I give is that which I have.

Through my whole-hearted giving, I *make room* for an ever-increasing good to express through me. The law of unfoldment is now active in my life. All limiting thoughts that I can impoverish myself through giving are rendered powerless as I realize the limitlessness of God-substance and *its flow* through me. I am a channel through which God gives of Itself to life in specific ways. God is not limited. I will not limit Its givingness. I stretch out my hand to give and, as that gift is received under the law of balance and unfoldment, *my hand is filled to overflowing* as it returns to my side.

❧ Today, as I make room for that good which I desire. Spirit within me, as me, knows what I should do, how I should give of myself in order to receive. There is no wasted effort and joy accompanies my giving. A sense of freedom engulfs me. The freedom of God-life moves harmoniously through me. As I give, I partake of the Divine nature of self-givingness.

Through giving, this day and every day, I bless myself and others.

THIS MOMENT I EXPRESS JOY

"These things have I spoken unto you, that my joy might remain in you, and that your joy might be full."

–John 15:11

There is One Life and that life is God-life. I am aware of God as my life, constantly expressing through me as my objective environment and physical well-being, creating my experiences according to my *belief* and *acceptance*.

Right now, I accept all of the good, the just, and the true from my past experience. In this present moment I enter into the mental atmosphere of the joy of all past experiences knowing they set the pattern for my *present* and *future* well-being. There are no negative comparisons, no seeking to perpetuate any given past experience. There is no living in the past for me. There is no desire to live in the past; I live only in the now. My experience of living is controlled by the past at this moment only to the degree that I accept it. To me is given the prerogative of self-choice. Through this *divine gift*, I control my thought, feelings, and destiny. I seek always to choose wisely, positively, and affirmatively.

☙ Right now I accept only the good from all experience, and this good multiplies itself in everything I do. My life at this moment is orderly and freed from the influence of all past undesirable happenings. In the joy of this moment, I am alive to the presence of Infinite Spirit as *love* and *right action* moving through me, calming, assuring, and vitalizing me in every way. The future is filled only with good and happiness. This is the *best* moment in my life. I am happy and rejoice in it. In harmony, order, peace, and courage I move with the present through eternity.

I TRUST THE INTEGRITY OF LOVE

*"Commit thy way unto the Lord; trust also in him;
and he shall bring it to pass."*

—Psalms 37:5

*T*oday, and in the *inner quietness* of this moment, all feeling of weight and oppression slips from my mind. Unhappy or past hurtful experiences, lack of self-confidence, and oppressive thoughts all fade into nothingness as through understanding love my eyes are opened. I see these events and thoughts now, not as things in themselves, but only as my limited concept and acceptance of things. There is a *basic integrity* at the center of God-life, and that center is everywhere present. Nothing is ever out of balance in the absoluteness of God. As I realize my oneness with Infinite Mind, I know that there is a presence within me that will always direct me.

The activity of Spirit within me leads me into paths of peace and right action as I turn to It in confidence and faith. Regardless of appearances, I know there are not two opposing powers as good and evil, health and sickness, abundance and poverty. This illusion disappears as I realize, now, the basic goodness and integrity of God-mind. My awareness of this enables me to assume dominion over my life. I consciously move with the stream of life, knowing that God-life can be trusted.

With an ease of mind, I now quietly turn from that which disturbs to the contemplation of the Presence within me; to the wonderful power of God-life waiting to pour itself through me according to my bidding.

This day, in *faith* and *trust* in the integrity of God, which is love, I assume dominion over all apparent negation.

I AM IMPELLED TO RIGHT ACTION

"Heaven and earth shall pass away, but my words shall not pass away."

–Matthew 24:35

*T*oday I speak my word for right action in all things that I think, do, and say. Right action means constructive action. All that I do brings greater harmony of thought, experience, and opportunity for self-giving into my life. In all my associations with others, there is only harmony and good, and I am open and receptive to Divine ideas.

The pure essence of Divine ideas flow through me at all times, because I have a *willingness* to *let* it be so. I have no sense of strain or force in becoming the channel through which right action works. Water flows through provided channels according to the activity of the law of gravity. So does the spirit of harmony move through me, according to Spiritual law as I remove the obstructions of fear, doubt, misunderstanding, and strain.

This day I let go of any past negative experiences. I do not have to force them out of my mind. They lose their power as I become more aware of my Oneness with Infinite Spirit–the realm of divine ideas. Calmly, now, I turn to the inherent goodness of God-life and let right action move through me and out into all that I do. Only constructive and helpful ideas about myself and others claim my attention.

ᐭ This word I now speak provides the way for Divine law to produce right action in my experience. This word is the law unto its own fulfillment. Knowing I am One with the Allness of God, I let the impulsion of the Divine guide, direct, and compel me into paths of right action, now and always.

I AM CONSTANTLY IN MY RIGHT PLACE

*"But whoso looketh into the perfect law of liberty,
and continueth therein...this man shall be blessed
in his deed."*

–James 1:25

Everything in the universe is in a state of *perfect balance* according to the Law of Infinite Intelligence. Perfect harmony is everywhere present. Nothing can ever be out of order or misplaced in the eyes of God. This means that while there is constant change, as a creative process takes place, there is an *immediate readjustment* to maintain perfect balance.

God's law of harmony and love is constantly working through me as I move from experience to experience. If at times I seem to be maladjusted or not expressing according to what I feel reflects my highest capabilities, in reality I know I can never be out of my true and rightful place. Although it may seem as though I am not where I should be, this cannot be true about my *real self*. It is only when I think of any particular activity in my life as being fixed or static, that I give it power to make me unhappy. As I come to realize I am One with God and Its activity of harmony, desirable readjustments take place in my life, leading to an outward manifestation of joyous, happy and satisfying self-fulfillment.

❧ Today, I rightly view all experience, knowing that I am in my right place according to the law of my being. No experience is fixed or static. Therefore, I do not fight my present experience. According to my belief, it is done unto me. This day I know new opportunities come to me as I mentally embrace a greater good. Spirit within me lovingly guides and directs me into paths of *richer opportunity*. I *listen* closely, with a willingness to be led into expressions of greater achievement and good. This unfolding process is constantly at work in my life. I am in my right place, now and forevermore.

CLEAR THINKING IS MY DIVINE BIRTHRIGHT

"...Whatsoever things are true... honest... just...
pure...lovely...of good report; if there be any virtue,
and if there be any praise, think on these things."
—Philippians 4:8

Clarity of thought is God-created and God-intended in every person. Thought is the activity of Spirit, and Infinite Spirit is the great Source and potential of all ideas. The movement of Intelligence or Spirit becomes crystallized as thought or mind's self-awareness within me. We did not create ourselves, neither did we create the God-given attribute of *thinking* or *self-awareness*. Each individual is an active, *creative, focalizing* center of the Mind-Divine. We awaken to self-awareness through some act of God within ourselves. Through our self-awareness, we are able to function intelligently in the objective and relative experience of our environment. It is only as we give too much undue importance to external things, particularly if they are of a negative nature, and we become confused and muddled in our thinking. Things of themselves never have power over the individual. It is only one's inner reaction to, or feeling about, things and events that causes confusion of thought. Clear thinking is assuming dominion over one's reaction to that which is going on around one. Clear thinking is the natural movement of Infinite Spirit through Its creation. As we realize more fully our Oneness with God and know that in reality Spirit cannot be confused, we gain the wisdom and insight that enable us to assume dominion over our distorted thought. There is someplace within our mind that never was confused or disturbed, nor can be. As we continue to affirm this and through love give our attention to something of a more harmonious nature, our divine birthright of clear thinking will follow.

❧ This day, I become more aware of my oneness with all of life. The Spirit of God in me, as me, cannot be confused, misjudged, or be disturbed by objective conditions or happenings. At all times I turn with confidence to the kingdom of God within me. The wisdom and love of Infinite Spirit envelops my consciousness, and I am peaceful and harmonious in my thinking.

INCREASING FAITH IS MINE

*"And all things, whatsoever ye shall ask in prayer,
believing, ye shall receive."*

–Matthew 21:22

Faith is that attitude of mind which *knows*. It is a complete acceptance wherein there is no *doubt*, even though the intellect does not comprehend all the details. God or Infinite Mind cannot know anything other than perfect faith, since God cannot know anything other than Itself. God has endowed us with all the faith we shall ever need, for "I and my Father are one."

To us there seems to be different *levels* of faith. Our faith appears to be conditioned by our past experience and thinking. We have perfect faith in those things that we can accept or with which we are familiar. Constantly, we are reaping the harvest of this level of faith in our outward experiences. To achieve greater things, we must raise our level of acceptance.

As we realize our Oneness with God and feel that God is in us, through us, and for us, we immediately begin to embody a greater faith. This expanded vision and acceptance causes us to realize that it is not necessary or important that we know all the answers ahead of time. As we learn to trust the integrity of God and life, even in *small* ways, our faith increases.

❧ This day, I have all the faith I shall need. In many ways I see this trust justified. As I contemplate my use of faith, even in apparently small ways, and realize my Oneness with God, the Infinite Source, increasing faith is mine. The Life-Principle guides my mind and controls my body. While my intellect agrees with and, through cooperation with this Life-Principle, *permits* these things to happen, something greater that I am *causes* them to happen. It is my faith in this unseen something greater that enables me to say, "There is a Presence and a Power within me that responds to my thought." At this moment, as I realize the full meaning of this statement, my faith is increased and I accept my good.

THIS DAY IS A GOOD DAY

"It is a good thing to give thanks unto the Lord,
and to sing praises unto thy name, O Most High."
—Psalms 92:1

*T*his day is a *new beginning*. I am filled with joyous expectancy, knowing that all I do this day shall bring joy, happiness, love and a sense of well-being to me and all whom I contact.

Any negations, anxieties, and confusions of past experiences slip into nothingness as I accept that each day is a new beginning. This day I accept only the good, the true, the beautiful, and the lovely from past experiences. As I move into this day's experiences, I know they shall be the *patterns* for an ever-increasing receptivity of greater good in my life. This realization is fruitful. It is my word that goes before and paves the way, as I acknowledge and accept that it is, in reality and in Truth, the word of Spirit speaking through me for my highest good. I accept this truth in faith. Spirit leads me from moment to moment wisely and productively. I gently brush from my mind any thought of past failure or unhappiness that may try to assert itself. Any doubt of my ability, usefulness, or worth is instantly rendered impotent as I, with a deep feeling of love, enter into the spirit of the great adventure of richer living, today.

In each experience this day, I look for and see greater opportunity of service to others. As this sense of love and well-being moves out from me to all life, I know that I meet it returning to me wherever I go and in whatever I do. For me and for all whom I contact, *this day is a good day*. It is indeed good to be alive and I thrill to the harmonious rhythm of life within me. So shall it be this day and forever.

"Love and do what you like."
–St. Augustine